LIVING IN THE SHADOW OF BEING THE BEST FRIEND OF MARSHALL FAULK HALL OF FAME INDUCTEE

The True Story of Two Childhood Friends
Mark Bruno and Marshall Faulk

This is a riveting story of how two childhood friends shared coming of age experiences in New Orleans' Infamous Ninth Ward (Desire Housing Projects). The story details how the two boys overcome an environment riddled with crime, violence and depravity as they escape the streets of New Orleans. This story details Marshall Faulk's rise to Glory and his friend's fall from grace.

Mark Bruno

Order this book online at www.trafford.com
or email orders@trafford.com

Most Trafford titles are also available at major online book retailers.

Printed in the United States of America.

ISBN: 978-1-4669-1657-9 (sc)
ISBN: 978-1-4669-1656-2 (e)

Trafford rev. 03/06/2012

 www.trafford.com

North America & international
toll-free: 1 888 232 4444 (USA & Canada)
phone: 250 383 6864 ♦ fax: 812 355 4082

CONTENTS

DEDICATION TO MY MOTHER

This book is written in Loving Memory of my mother Alcebia Catherine Bruno better known as "Ms. Sibby".

DOCUMENTATION OF MY STORY

articles on mark bruno best friend of

About 61,100 results (0.24 seconds)

Matthew Hinton/The Times-Picayune

Marshall Faulk, a former star football player at Carver who grew up in the Desire housing development, will become the first New Orleans native to be inducted into the Pro Football Hall of Fame.

Star runner Marshall Faulk of the Colts has rushed to the - 07.24.95 ...

Jul 24, 1995 – Star runner **Marshall Faulk** of the Colts has rushed to the place where he's ... By his senior year Marshall was spending most of his time outside of school with his best friend, **Mark Bruno**. ... ARTICLES, GALLERIES, COVERS ...

Marshall Faulk had the will and the desire to better himself and his ...

Aug 2, 2011 – "**Marshall** is so special," said **Mark Bruno**, Faulk's childhood best friend. "Only one out of a million can do what he has done coming where we ...

Marshall Faulk's run to daylight

Jul 31, 2011 – **Marshall Faulk** celebrates his first one yard touchdown run against the Vikings in the first quarter. ... So here is the best story teller of them all. ..... named **Mark Bruno**, whose family cared enough to bring Faulk into their home for ...

A town named Desire Faulk runs from rugged projects to Super Bowl ...

Jan 31, 2002 – **Article** Collections ... Faulk has tried his best this week to avoid questions about his rough upbringing. He doesn't want ... best friend, **Mark Bruno**, served one year for theft. ... Well, **Marshall** knew where he wanted to go ...

Not That Easy - Los Angeles Times

Jan 27, 2002 – Faulk, Stewart Had Some Rough Years in New Orleans, but Now It Looks ... LOUIS — They vowed to escape New Orleans, but now, a decade later, **Marshall Faulk** and Kordell Stewart will do just about ... for armed robbery, and his best friend from high school, **Mark Bruno**, got ... Los Angeles Times Articles ...

ORANGE AND GREEN - (NEW ORLEANS, LA) - powered by ...

"**Marshall** is so special," said **Mark Bruno**. Faulk's childhood best friend. "Only one out of a million can do what he has done coming where we come from. ...

Mark Bruno/best friend of
Marshall Faulk

ARTICLES   SI COVERS   PHOTO GALLERIES

July 24, 1995

Babying Himself

Star runner Marshall Faulk of the Colts has rushed to the place where he's most comfortable—the lap of luxury

John Ed Bradley

View this issue

PRINT   EMAIL   MOST POPULAR   SHARE

1   2   3   4   5   6   7   8   9   10   11

"You would never know who he is in a room of 30 or 40 people," Marchibroda says. "And he wouldn't want you to know. He doesn't care to be the center of attention—that's the sort of person he is. He's very confident and aware, but at the same time he's humble. He has the actions of an older person, and this is one of the things I find most interesting about him. He was 28 last year when he was 21." By his senior year Marshall was spending most of his time outside of school with his best friend, Mark Bruno. When Cecile moved from the Desire project to another troubled, though less benighted, area of the city, Reese persuaded her to allow Marshall to stay near Carver. Soon after, he moved in with the Brunos. "It wasn't a project house," Mark says, "but right on the corner—real close, you know."

A town named Desire Faulk runs from rugged projects to Super Bowl

BY HANK GOLA

Thursday, January 31, 2002

NEW ORLEANS - The taxi pulled off the raised interstate onto a foreboding exit, past a desolate pocket of houses with patches of grass passing for lawns, past street corners where the drug deals start to percolate around nightfall.

Right over there they knocked down the infamous Desire Housing Project. The leveled landscape still makes up some of the most dangerous territory in the murder capital of the country.

"You're in the Ninth Ward," says the cabbie, "as in Nine Millimeter."

Another right turn and there it is: a sprawling mass of dark brick, chipped concrete, grimy windows and breezeways of rusting corrugated metal that promises all the comfort of Camp X-Ray.

This is George Washington Carver High School, the unlikely wellspring of Marshall Faulk's immense football talent.

A rose that blooms in the desert? A decade ago, Faulk was a Carver Ram. This week he is back home, leading the St. Louis Rams into the Super Bowl as arguably the best football player in the world.

Faulk has tried his best this week to avoid questions about his rough upbringing. He doesn't want kids to think the only way out of here is football.

"It has nothing to do with where I grew up," he says. "There are other people who grew up in rough environments and you just don't hear about it. They make it in business ... they're doctors, they're lawyers. But we're not talking about that.

"I don't think that makes me what I am. What makes me what I am is that you keep your head on straight and make the right decisions in life. I didn't always walk the straight line. I'm not going to say that I'm an angel. But I made some right decisions along the way."

Others who lived in the Desire Projects didn't. One of Faulk's three brothers was sentenced to seven years in prison for armed robbery. His best friend, Mark Bruno, served one year for theft.

Faulk's parents divorced when he was four and when his mother, Cecile, couldn't make enough as a hotel maid and store clerk, she sent Marshall to live with the Brunos.

INTRODUCTION

This book is meant to welcome you the reader into my world as I struggled with living in the shadow of being the best friend of Marshall Faulk. I will take you on a journey from my childhood and coming of age experiences that were shared between myself and Marshall Faulk. This book will highlight the highs and lows of Marshall's Career as a NFL Football Player and the highs and lows that I experienced as his friend. Welcome to my world, Mark Bruno the best friend of Marshall Faulk, Hall of Fame Inductee.

CHAPTER 1

CHILDHOOD

Well, where can I start? Back in the days growing up in the Desire Housing Projects, there were these two adolescent kids by the name of Mark and Marshall. These two guys were distinguished and stood out from the rest of the kids. Now don't get me wrong, there were a lot of smart and bright kids, with lots of potential. These kids all had the potential of being something one day. One must take into account the environment these kids live in on a daily basis. The Ninth Ward's Desire Projects was a place where murders took place almost every day. There was not only crime and violence, but the two came from a part of town where families did not have much and they struggled to make ends meet. Even facing poverty and adversity, their families managed to make it. This book will show you how these two young men and childhood friends rose above the obstacles and overcame becoming a product of their bad environment. Many of their friends did not make it. Some of them ended up on drugs, going to jail and even went to an early grave. They relied on a true bond, friendship, faith in God a will and determination to become somebody one day.

Mark: What's up Marshall, hey man are you going to practice today? Marshall: Yeah, but I have to hurry up and finish my homework first. Mark: Man you should have done that in class, like I've been doing so you wouldn't have to rush to finish for practice. You can just take your time in class. Marshall: I know man that's what I usually do I was just tripping today messing around with Patrice. Anyway dog, I'll be there. I shouldn't be too late. Mark: Alright buddy I'll see you at practice.

It was about 3:30 pm on a beautiful sunny afternoon in the neighborhood park. The park was called The Great Sampson Park. Sampson Park was a place where a lot of true athletic stars were born and a lot of young men were molded and reared to tough young men. Sampson Park kept a lot of us out of a lot of trouble because of the activities that was offered to us at the park. There were football, basketball and baseball teams. If it wasn't for that park, I seriously don't think that I would be alive today to write this book. Now let's get back to the script. Coach Rabbit: Bruno, you're late! Give me two laps. Where's Marshall? Mark: Umm, umm he said he would be a few minutes late. Oh, there he is crossing the neutral ground (A neutral ground is small patch of a grassy area in the middle of the street). As Marshall crossed the neutral ground Mark pointed him out to coach. Coach Rabbit: Hurry up Marshall. You and Bruno give me two laps. You guys are the captains of the team. You should be setting a good example for the rest of the team. Don't let it happen again. Alright coach, replied Mark and Marshall. The two boys finished a full day of practice. Their team was known as Pop Warners Little League Athletes. As their athletic careers began to evolve who would have known that one of the two would make it as a star athlete, go onto be an MVP player and later be inducted into Football Hall of Fame. During this time the two guys attend different schools and have not seen much of each other. They both continue to live in the same neighborhood and remain true to their dreams as athletes. The two are reunited years later as they enter high school.

CHAPTER 2

THE BEGINNING

The beginning, four years later. Mark and Marshall were still the best of friends. No longer little boys, now the two have grown to be two respectable young men. They have developed a reputation as athletes. Something was special about the boys, they had charisma. They had a certain way of dressing, people knew that they were athletes and they were adored by the girls as well as the school staff. Everyone knew that they were destined for greatness. The young men have now reached their freshmen year. Everybody could feel it. Mark and Marshall had special talents. Who would have imagined, these two guys would make it out of the hood. These guys were up against a lot of odds. Their environment did not change, but these guys were being developed as athletes in the middle of the hood. In the midst of it all, the two guys had an agreement. They always believed that one of them would make it out of the hood. So there it was the agreement. If one made it out of the hood, he would be the one to help the other bring him and his family out of the hood. They depended on each other to bring about a brighter future for their families.

Likewise, the guys shared almost everything. Journey with me as the story unfolds. Marshall: What's up Iya? Mark: What's up man? Can you believe we are going to be freshmen in high school? Marshall: Yeah man we're getting up there. Next thing you I know we're going to be seniors and graduating and going on to college. Mark: I know man. I can't wait for those days to come either. I already have my mind made up. I'm going straight to Georgetown on a Basketball Scholarship. Next, straight to the Pro's. I see it now New Jersey Nets selects Mark Bruno number one pick in the draft. Marshall: Yeah man you got big dreams. That's good, you know ya boy is behind you one hundred percent. But for now Spud Web, let's just get out of high school. Mark: You're right. Man don't hate, I gotcha. Speaking of dreams, what are your plans for the future? Marshall: Well to tell you the truth man, I haven't really thought about it. There is one thing I do know, I would like to make my momma proud by going to college and graduating with a degree. I want my momma to have things she has never had. I just hate to see my momma struggling all the time. Always going to or coming from work. I am going to make that change for my mother. She deserves better. Mark: I feel you dog. I am right there with you. I want the same for my moms too. Well you still have time, I mean; we still have time to figure it all out. We still have a whole life ahead of us. Who knows what the future holds. Marshall: And you're right. The two guys are now sitting on the front porch, where they spent most of their time. They were looking into a glimpse of their future. They both had dreams of an athletic career. They knew that this would be their ticket out of the hood. They knew their families could have and live better. They were going to make it happen.

The Front Porch

They were dreaming big. But just as hard as they dreamed, they worked even harder. Now, these guys were not just athletes, they also learned how to hustle. Hustle, I don't mean anything illegal. Now, everybody in the hood had some kind of hustle. People sold candy and drinks from their back doors. People had hair salons in their homes. These two guys, they were barbers. As barbers, we had a lot of competition. Each barber was known for the kind of cut he provided. The Bruno kid was known for cutting a lightning bolt in the side of your bald fade. I was good. I mean really good. So I taught Marshall the trade. We made two dollars a cut. We cut hair right from my mother's front porch. This was our way to keep some fresh kicks or nice pair of Gerbaud Jeans. Man, just think of how much money I would be making today if I had stayed in that line of work.

Moreover, there were some other good neighborhood barbers as well. Mark and Marshall were in competition with some of the best if not the best neighborhood barbers. There was one barber by the name of Calvin. Calvin was a beast at cutting hair. He was known for cutting almost everybody's hair in the Desire Projects. He could draw anything in your head. He could put any design in your head and I mean any. There was yet another barber by the name of

Roland. Roland picked up where Calvin left off. Roland put a new spin on cutting hair, he had a signature cut. A beast at cutting hair, the two guys ran a close race in determining who the best at cutting hair was. In those days, these two guys were my role model barbers. I had not perfected my skill with the hair designs these guys had accomplished. Marshall and I still stood in our lane as it pertained to cutting hair. I could cut a mean bald fade with my signature lightning bolt. I don't cut hair to that magnitude of clientele that I had in those days, but I'm still a beast at what I do. Ya dig!

Ms Sibby

Moving along, now that porch wasn't just a place for cutting hair and a place to reminisce my mom played a significant role with the neighborhood kids. When we sat on that porch, we had to be on our best behavior. My mom was always there to correct anyone who got out of line. If the fellows used foul language or got into confrontations my mother would stop them. My mother was known as Ms. Sibby: to the fellows. Even though she was a source of discipline, she showed everybody Love. Ms. Sibby: Mark and Marshall, are you guys hungry? Talking to the fellows as she leaned on the screened door she asked if they wanted to eat. I just finished cooking a hot meal. Yeah, mom. What did you cook? Ms. Sibby, replied to the boy, I just finished cooking some pork chops and macaroni with peas on the side. I cooked your favorite meal. Mark: Momma you ain't saying nothing. Hell Yeah, we're hungry! Ms. Sibby asked the other guys on the porch if they were hungry as well.

In all actuality Marshall became part of our family. Now during this time Marshall's family was going through some financial problems as well as his mother being sick. Hell, we all were going through some money problems. When you live in the hood, that's just a given. Marshall's situation was just a little bit worst than the usual problem. His situation had gotten so bad, that his mother allowed him to move in with our family. This wasn't an easy task. Let's look at what really happened.

Marshall's mother had some financial problems. Marshall was a part of a large family. He had five brothers. His father did not play a major role in providing for the family. His mother, Ms. Cecile had five mouths to feed. One could imagine that this would be a hardship on any mother. Next, thing we found out that Marshall was moving across the river. Now, we had begun practicing over the summer for football practice. Marshall started having problems getting back and forth to and from practice. He started sleeping at different friends houses. During this time me and Marshall began to grow closer as friends. He would spend a lot of time at our house. The more Marshall struggled to get to and from practice every day, the more Coach Reese started to notice. This led Marshall and I to the conclusion that he should move into the Bruno family home. Now, this was no easy task. I had to convince my mother, who was also struggling financially to allow Marshall to live with us. This meant she had a new mouth to feed. Marshall would be another teenager to be concerned about and to keep out of trouble. My mother, being the person she was at the time after much persuasion agreed to allow Marshall to live with us. Marshall became a part of our family. We grew close as brothers. I actually saw Marshall as the brother I never had. We were willing to share our home with Marshall. Remember, we live in the hood. In New Orleans, people live in what you call shotgun houses. These houses were like doubles, but the difference is that a shotgun house you can stand in the front door and see clean through to the back door. If you opened the front door and opened the back door, you could see the trees in the backyard. We didn't just live in a shotgun house it was a two bedroom shack. We were thankful for what we had, but it was a sacrifice we were willing to make. We had a kitchen, a living room, a bathroom and two rooms. I shared one of those rooms with Marshall. My sister, Monique lost the independence of her bed and had to share a bed with my mom in the other room of the house. Well Marshall officially became a family member. Believe me our family had struggles just as Marshall's family had experienced but we made it through it all. Additionally, Mark and Marshall were almost inseparable. If you saw Mark then you would soon see Marshall and vice versa. These guys were like brothers. We often balled in the neighborhood center. We also had certain people we would hang out with. These guys all had special talents. I mentioned this earlier, we were some special guys. There were a lot of kids that had potential of making it out of the hood and becoming someone great. We had friends like George, my little cousin Courtney, my boy Milton, my boy Darryl better known as Snot Box. These are just to name a few I could go and on, but they know who they are. These guys all could be found in the neighborhood center on one day or the other.

The Center

Man I wonder if George is home, asked Mark? Come on Marshall let's go see if that dude is home. He might want to go and play some ball with us at the center. Approaching George's house, which was right next door Mark began to call out for George. Oh George, Oh George. Just to mention, George and Mark were close friends as well. They lived next door to each other and they shared a special bond. Their relationship could be compared to the one he shared with Marshall. George was a real talented guy. He had game. George had hops. He was the LeBron James mixed with a little Michael Jordan of our time in the hood. When I tell you this guy had hops out of this world. I literally mean it. George was an unbelievable basketball player. He had the skills and the talent to go to any division one college. He had the potential to go pro. George was one of the first dudes I ever seen to perform the "rocking cradle dunk", just like Michael Jordan. One of Michael Jordan's patterned dunks. George had anyone who watched him play in amazement. To tell you the truth George was the most athletic one of us all. You know what y'all, like I said before the hood can rob you of all your potential and change your destiny. The hood got a hold of old George and took him under. He ended up on drugs and turned into someone I did not recognize. Like Donnie McClurkin says in a song "We fall down, but we get up" (2001). A lot of true soldiers came out of the ninth ward area, I guess that's the way were built to overcome adversity. We will talk about that later. For now let's continue.

Knock, knock, knock George replies, who is it. Mark: It's me man, Mark. As George opens the door, Mark replies, what's up fool. George: Man, what's up. Mark: Marshall and I are heading over to the Center, you want to roll. George: Yeah man, hold up while I change my gear. I need to change into something I can ball in. I would let y'all in, but you know how moms be tripping. Y'all just wait right here and I'll be right back.

Now the center was a common ground, a place that kept a lot of us out of trouble. The center was the spot where most of us came to let off a lot of steam and frustration on the basketball court. We didn't just go to the center to let off steam, but we went to the center to display our love of the game of basketball and our competitiveness. Now playing in the center, you couldn't just be the average Joe. Playing in the center, you had come with it. You had to be a serious baller. Your game on the court had to be vicious. In there and in those days, we really lived for the game. We had basketball in our blood. It wasn't a joke. You had to be serious about the game or you could just go home. Those guys were so good they would shame you in front of your momma. You would not want to come out of the summer if you did not come with your 'A' game in the center. The center had schedule and most teens showed up for what was known as "free play". During this time, free play was open gym. Each team played half court games and whichever team reached twelve first was the winner. There was a long line of players waiting for winners. That is, they would be the next up to hit the court to play the winners. In the center, was a common ground it didn't matter which walk of life you came from. When you stepped in the center it was all about the game of basketball and winning. You could have been a murderer, a drug dealer, a pimp or whatever stepping through those doors all images and stereotypes went out the window. It was all about the game of basketball. Imagine, back in those days, some guys would come into the gym with guns and drama on their jacket. Guess what nothing that went on outside transpired inside of the gym. We had some strict coaches and they were not having it. The rules were followed. Once you left the center it was back to reality. Everybody went back into character. If you were a pimp you back to the game, if a pusher you went back to the corner, if a robber you are back masked up or whatever your character may have been you went back to it. Man, there was no place like the center. Some of these guys could have been bankers, lawyers, pharmacists and accountants but many of these guys have been robbed of their potential. Let's get back to the script.

While we stood outside of George's house, he finally came out and ready to go ball. George had changed his gear and was ready. George: Y'all ready? Marshall: Yeah man, you took long enough. As the three of us began to walk towards the center, a voice shouted from the distance. Mark, Marshall, George, wait up, yelled Courtney. This was my little cousin Courtney. He was one who almost lost all of his potential in the hood. Courtney was the baby of the bunch and we were his role models. Now when I say he was the baby of the bunch, I mean he was the youngest and he really thought he was in our age group. When I say he was the baby I don't mean that he was soft or anything. He was one of us, and he just knew that he was our age. At times, I would forget just how young he was. He was a part of our click. Now Courtney was a little soldier at heart, to say he was so young he was able to fit into the click. I forgot he was just a youngster. He still had a lot to learn about being in the hood. Courtney was like my little shadow. Courtney watched our every move. He soaked up everything we knew about the streets. At the time, we were really setting some bad examples for Courtney. Growing up in the hood that was all we knew. We thought that we were right, but we were only surviving in the hood. Now looking back, I would have set better examples for Courtney. That is, if I would have only known better. Like I say, the hood will rob you of your potential. He got caught up and ended up catching a case. He was emerged into the penal system. His experience with the penal system did not last a long time. He bounced back to the person I knew he was. Let's get back to the story. Courtney: What's up man? Mark: Man, we are on our way to the center. We are going play some ball, you coming? Courtney: Yeah man, I'm going to roll with y'all. As we walked down the middle of the street, we heard a beeping noise. Beep, beep, beep, it was the sound of Courtney's beeper. We all turned and looked at Courtney. Courtney raised his hands in the air and replied, "Man that's a sale." "I'm gon catch you fellows later." I'm trying to get paid, replied Courtney. When I tell you, that hustling seed was implanted in his blood, whatever he does he knows how to make money from it. Marshall: I hear you lil brother, be careful. Do yo thang. Mark: Courtney you better slow ya role, you moving too fast brah. Courtney: I'm straight dog. I'm just on the grind right now. Now can you imagine this lil dude was just fourteen and getting it in at an early age? He was in love with the game and fascinated by the bling, bling and fancy things. Now this is the driving force behind most of us in the hood. Well how can I knock him, he was a reflection of me. We all wanted things we did not have. We all were trying to achieve those things we saw on TV. on a daily basis. That's how so many kids were taken under by the hood. They get lost in the misconception of what life is all about. Well we live and learn. Even as kids Marshall and I was not happy about what we saw.

On the other hand, Marshall and I understood why he was the way he was. This was a survival strategy for living in the hood. He was only surviving in the streets the best way he knew how. Marshall: Mark what are you going to do with that lil dude. Man you have created a beast. Mark: Man y'all can't just blame me. We all played a part in molding Courtney. Just because that's my cousin doesn't mean that it's all my fault. You guys played a part as well. We did things in front of him, we had no business doing. He learned from what he saw. George: Yeah, dog your right. We exposed Courtney to too much at an early age. We should not have let him hang around us so much. We can't forget he is still a youngster. Mark: On a good note, at least he is not going to be a buster. At least he knows how to take care of his self. Marshall: Yeah Mark, that's positive thinking. He replied in a sarcastic voice. Mark: For real dog, you know how it is out here. Think about it. We are all living in these streets, living this life. How can we expect him to do any different when we were setting bad examples for him? Growing up in the hood were some wild days. I can honestly say we were some little thugs laced in the game. We were literally becoming products of our environment.

If it had not been for being involved in athletics as an outlet, the neighborhood would have taken us under as well. Our hood was bad, but not all bad. We learned a lot of life lessons in our hood. Growing up in the hood we had love for each other. We developed some true friendships and close bonds that even the waters of Hurricane Katrina couldn't break. Who knew in time what the future had in store for us. Journey with me.

Carver Rams High School Dance (1987-1991)
From Left to Right: Derrick Roby, Marshall Faulk, Mark Bruno,
Edward Morgan. Center : Kevin Roby

CHAPTER 3

HIGH SCHOOL YEARS

Now freshman at George Washington Carver High School, new coming of age experiences begin for the boys. Marshall, Mark and George remain close friends. Deep into sports, they were athletes at heart. In spite of all the negative things they did in the hood, these guys were taking a new direction in their lives. They were no longer boys; they were now developing as young men.

Now this is the first day of school. In those days, you had to make sure you were on point with your gear. That is, you had to make sure when you went to school your clothes made a statement. After all this was setting the standard for the school year. It's 7:30 am. Mark is getting ready for school. He is dressing for the day. His wardrobe includes a fresh blue Polo Shirt, a navy blue pair of Girbaud Jeans and pair of Addidas Forums. In those days that was a fashion statement. These were the hottest clothes anyone could find on Canal Street. Now Canal Street, that's another story. This was the fashion industry for the New Orleans culture. You had stores like Krauss, Woolworth's, Foot Locker, Maison Blanche, Gauchaux's,

Rubenstein Brothers, All American Jeans, Canal Place, D.H. Holmes just to name a few. One thing about living in New Orleans, you had to come with it. New Orleans has always been a fashion show. Dressing is a way of life for the people who live in New Orleans. We grew up a part of that culture. Back to the first day of school. Knock, knock, knock the sound came from the side of the Bruno's shotgun house. Mark: Who is it? Marshall: It's me Marshall. What's up man, you ready for school? Mark: Hell yeah! Marshall: Man you aren't even dressed. Mark: I was about to get dressed until you knocked on the door. Come on in man. Marshall: Man what are you going to wear? Mark: Man you already know, fresh Polo and the Girbaud's I bought on Canal Street yesterday. Marshall: Man you are just copying my style. As Mark gets dressed, Marshall profiles in the mirror checking him out. He glances over his outfit. He wore a red Polo, a pair of blue Giraud's and a fresh pair of red Bally Animals. That was the cream of the crop of shoe brands in New Orleans at that time. I don't know how, but Marshall and Mark managed to keep a top notch wardrobe.

These guys were from the hood. They both had single parents living off of limited incomes. Their homes were headed by their mothers who were the only source of income for their families. Most kids living in the hood may sometimes have a father, but nine times out of ten, they were out of work or were not there. Their mothers had to be strong and in many cases were the strength of their families. Marshall had it a little better than Mark. After all, he had four brothers to share clothes with. He also shared a lot of gear with Mark, one of his closest friends. Marshall: Man come on it's the first day of school dog. We have to get there early to get our shine on. Man, hurry up! Mark: I'm coming now, dog. I just have to put my shoes on! At the time it wasn't about going to school to get an education. For us, it was about getting your shine on. Who was going to be the flyest during those first few days of school? As they walked out of the door, you could see their school in a clear view from Mark's house. Mark stayed damn near across the street from Carver. You could get to school with a hop, skip and a jump from Mark's house. That's just how close Mark stayed to the school. You could see all of the kids migrating to school like a herd of cattle. It also resembled Fat Tuesday, Mardi Gras Day. On Mardi Gras Day people never travel cars. They generally walk everywhere they go on that day. That's just as an example of how many students attended Carver. As I mentioned earlier, George lived right next door to Mark. As Mark and Marshall proceeded to walk down the stairs of the front porch, George simultaneously met them in the middle of the street as they joined the large herd of students migrating to school. While walking to school George, Mark and Marshall engaged in a conversation about their outfits. George: Y'all boys are on point huh? Fresh Polo, fresh Giraud's, Bally's and all huh? Mark: You already know. For sho, you heard me. Marshall: Man this dude copied my style. Mark: Man I was on Canal Street all day yesterday. I know for sho I was the first one out there. George, what's happening with yo gear. Man you could have called me I had a fresh Polo shirt I could've gave you to wear to match that fit you have on. Holler at me tomorrow dog, I got you. George was a little less fortunate than we were. When it came to our gear, Marshall and I managed to keep top notch name brands outfits. We managed to keep up with the best of the best. Not saying we were rich or anything, but George wasn't all the way on point with his gear at the time. You know what, that was one of the things that made us close as friends. When one was lacking on gear, we would share our clothes with each other. That way we would all shine. That's what I loved about our click we had each other's back in those days. Now the conversation shifts away from their clothes and they begin talking about their dreams.

The three guys begin their discussion about what they expect from their high school years. They actually talk about which sports they want to play. Mark: Man are you guys going out for the football team? George: Man, I'm trying out for the basketball team first. I want to see if I could be the first freshman to make the varsity team. Now being a part of the athletic department at Carver High meant a lot to the community. Some of the best players were a part of this team. If you were chosen to be a part of any team at Carver, you truly had to be ready. Marshall, Mark and George were truly ready. The Ninth Ward Community was truly behind the school's athletic department. The Ninth Ward was known for dominating the news for crime and violence and the athletic nature of the school was the communities' only opportunity to shine for the rest of the city. There were some great people that graduated from Carver and the educational system was also good. The school never got that recognition. Like I said, playing in any athletic sport was important to the school's community. This gave the parents, students and administration alike the opportunity to step away from the negative connotation that went along with being in the hood.

Being a Carver Ram meant taking pride not only in the school, but also taking pride in the community in which we were from. Let's get back to freshman year.

Furthermore, Marshall, Mark and George were involved in sports all of their lives these guys kept sports a part of their lives since the days of Pop Warner's team. Playing for Sampson Park was the place that planted the seeds of a true athletic spirit in each one of these guys. These guys had been involved with some kind of sport since the age of nine. Carver was the place where all of the skills they had developed from earlier years would be seen by everyone. These guys were about to embark upon an adventure that would define who they were as young men and later as adult men. Mark: Hey Marshall! Man they're having tryouts for the football team tomorrow. Are you trying out? Marshall: Man, I'm trying out for everything, football, track and basketball. What about you? Mark: Man, I ain't trying out for no track team, but I'm definitely trying out for basketball. Maybe, I will even try out for football. Man do you think I'm big enough to try out for varsity football? Marshall: It's not how big you are, but it's how big your heart is, and for someone who only weighs 96 lbs. you definitely are big enough. Man you are a lil beast. You have the skills to play with the best of them. Mark: Thanks man, I guess you're right. I'm gonna pass on football. I'm going out for the basketball team. Also, I think I will have a better chance and basketball is where my passion is. Marshall: Well, whatever you're comfortable with follow your heart. Mark: So now you're a preacher? Marshall: Nah, I'm just trying to be real. I would never guide you wrong. I also want to help you make the right decision. As the day goes on, they are excited about which classes on their schedule. They notice they only have one or two classes together and they try to get their schedules changed so they could have lunch during the same period. Overall, the guys are really just excited that they are in high school. They manage to adjust to life as high school freshmen.

The next few days, the boys concentrate on their tryouts. They are not as concerned about their clothing as they consider the team tryouts. After a good day of school, it's about 3:15 pm and the bell will be ringing soon. The boys are a little nervous as they think more and more about the tryouts and who they would be competing against to get the positions they want. They see each other in the halls on the way to the gym. Mark: What's up man? You ready? Mark looks at Marshall with a tense and serious look on his face. Marshall: Nothin' man, just ready to try out for the team? Mark: Did you bring some extra clothes to try out for the football team? I heard it rained during third period, so the field might be a little bit muddy today. Marshall: Man, I ain't worried about no mud. You know we play in the mud all the time in the projects. Mark: Word, brah. Marshall: But anyway, I have my gear. What about you? Mark: I brought a lil something. I also heard that there was a long line for tryouts and for the physical exam. The guys continued their conversation as they stood in the line to get in for football tryouts. They talked about everything, were they big enough for varsity? Would they make the team? What kind of position would they get? If they made the team would they be given the opportunity to play at all? All these questions they discussed with each other and some just were in their minds as they faced their first encounter with what they saw as true manhood.

These questions were justifiable, because Mark only weighed about 96 lbs at the age of 14, and Marshall weighed about 125 lbs. Marshall was a little bit beefier than Mark. He would fit in with the football team a little easier than Mark. The team had football players that looked like men with beards and all. Some of these guys were over six feet tall. Not to say that this was intimidating, but it was a factor to consider. These guys had just graduated from middle school and the kids they played against were somewhat under developed in many ways. As the guys got closer to the front of the line and they continued conversing, Mark decided that football was just not for him. These guys will kill me out there, replied Mark. He gave Marshall some dap. Mark: Man I see you later. I'm gon' be real, I still have some growing to do and a few more pounds to put on. Marshall: Man, I know you ain't punking out. Mark: Man, hell no. I'm just being real. I have some more growing to do and if I'm going to play sports, I have a better chance at basketball. With my height, I would be just what they're looking for as a point guard. Marshall: You do have a point. Mark: I'm going to give it a shot. I heard that Coach Reese is a good coach to play for. I heard he knows how to develop his players and bring out their true potential. Marshall: Go for it dog. Mark turns and heads out of the gym as Marshall watches his departure. The guys had made the decision on which sports they were going to participate in.

The decision to play football for Marshall and Mark's decision not to play football was the beginning of the path that their lives would take. Marshall lived with his family and Mark lived with his family. They played different sports, still managed to be the closest of friends. Marshall made the varsity football team. Just as the boys had suspected, as a freshman you hardly get a chance to play. Mark also made the varsity basketball team and he also experienced hardly ever playing. Either of the teams had not realized the true talent of either of these guys, but they were both stars in their own rights. Really Marshall didn't know what he had to offer and had not realized his true potential and neither did Mark. Marshall did not know what God had placed in him, the true gifts that lie on the inside of him. He had not tapped that true potential. It was like someone turned on the switch one day and he just started being the man that he was destined to be. We dreamed about going pro, but who would have ever thought that he would go to the NFL and go on to be a football hall of famer. This was outside of our wildest dreams. Let me show you how Marshall's abilities blew our minds. Even at a young age.

CHAPTER 4

A STAR IS BORN

On a cool winter night in Pan Am Stadium, the crowd packed in the bleachers for the Carver vs. Cohen Football Game. This was one of the biggest games of the season; Cohen was the number one rivalry team of the Carver Rams. This game could be compared to the New Orleans Saints against the Atlanta Falcons or Grambling versus Southern. Anyway it was the game of the season and we were getting psyched up about it at school all week. That's just how intense this game was for us. That's just how much pride the students and the rest of the community felt about the game. It was like uptown against downtown. Back in those days, the alumni and students took these games to heart. For the players, this night would be the night anyone of could shine. Everybody was looking. So any opportunity at any moment could determine your career path. Speaking of skills and opportunity this night would prove just who Marshall was as an athlete. Tonight a star would be born on that field. This night would be a defining moment in the life of Marshall Faulk. Of all the times I've watched Marshall play, this night would prove to me and everyone watching the skills that lie dormant inside of Marshall. This is the night that a true athlete and star is born.

Carver is down by five points, Cohen twenty one Carver sixteen. It is the fourth quarter with about twenty four seconds left in the game. Let's not forget that Marshall is just a freshman on the varsity team. During the game, the starting running back was hurt during the second quarter. This guy was a senior. The second strength running back twisted his ankle on the present snap of the ball with just seventeen seconds left in the game. Carver needs a miracle. Carver was at the ten yard line and needing ninety yards for a touchdown. They would have to pull a rabbit out of a hat or some other magic trick or move of heaven. Remember the two starting players were out of the game and hurt. There was no one left to put in the game but an unknown freshman. His skills had not been tested before this night. The coach took a chance and called on Marshall. He was a third string running back. All hope was gone, as so they thought. As the crowd waited in suspense, Coach Reese calls a time out. Not knowing what he would do next, Coach Reese huddled the team. He gives them an encouraging pep talk. Coach Reese: It's not over team; play with all of your heart. This school is depending on you to bring them into victory. As I watched with the rest of the Rams family, Coach turns to the crowd and shouts victory! He then looks intensely at Marshall and says strap up! Marshall nervously scrambles for his gear. He has never played in a high school game before this night. Marshall straps up, adrenaline flowing. Marshall jumped up and down warming up for the game in which there was only seconds left. Coach Reese designed a play we all were familiar with and termed it the "Hail Mary". Coach looks at Marshall and says, "I need you to block for Maurice." Maurice was the quarterback. Marshall replies, "Alright coach." As the time runs out, the team rushes back to the field you could feel the crowds' anticipation in the air. The entire stadium gets quiet. As the team lines up for the snap, Marshall never imagined that this would be the turning point of his life. As his friend, I witnessed with the rest of the Rams family a star being born. As the ball is snapped, Maurice drops back into the pocket, as the receiver broke and ran long towards the end zone. He had hoped to catch a Hail Mary. As the team members ran the routes, Maurice scrambles in the pocket. Marshall and Tyrone try their best to hold the defense off of the quarterback. Time is steadily ticking down. No one is open. Marshall and Tyrone can no longer hold off the defense. Marshall's defense slips pass him, almost sacking Maurice. Maurice with just an ounce of energy manages to get the ball off to Marshall with a little shuffle pass. Marshall unexpectedly catches the ball. He then turns and run the remaining ninety yards evasively eluding all tacklers as he graciously and fluently runs the ball. He ran that ball with style and agility; his body resembled that of a machine as he ran. His speed could be compared to that of a locomotive freight train. He took the crowd by storm. In that moment my friend transformed himself before my eyes. He resembled the great Erick Dickerson, someone we had both admired during that time. In that moment he had become one to be admired. He carried the Carver Rams to victory. Man that was a sight to see. Man I knew Marshall was good, but I didn't know he was that good. After the game everyone rallied around Marshall. They all were proclaiming how he resembled the great Erick Dickerson in his style of running the ball. He actually lived up to the expectation of being one of the best in the years following this incident. He became one of the best running backs to ever play the game of football.

Reflection

Destined to be great, Marshall was number thirty three, but he should have been number twenty nine. He was a mere reflection of the great Eric Dickerson. As the school year went on, Marshall developed and realized that football was his calling. Throughout the football season, game after game, Marshall started getting more and more playing time. His performance became more and more amazing. Coach Reese helped Marshall realize his full potential as a football player. He was the father figure he needed to mold him into the kind of man he is today. Coach Reese played a role in the life of Marshall Faulk like most other coaches. He was the driving force behind his development. There were many factors that attributed to Marshall's success, but at this moment Marshall's life started its own course to be the star that God had destined him to be. Keep in mind audience, that it wasn't easy. Marshall had a road ahead of him that many before him had not traveled. Marshall still had a lot to experience and a lot to learn.

In addition, he would get the opportunity throughout his school years to acquire more skills and abilities. Midway in Marshall's Sophomore Year in high school, Marshall was now a full blown super star as a football player. Marshall became an all around athlete.

Marshall played football, ran track and played on the basketball team. Some might not know, but Marshall was just as good in basketball as he was in football. Marshall and I went at it all of the time playing a friendly competitive game of basketball. We helped each other to develop and sharpen each other's athletic skills. I can honestly say, Marshall helped me develop my skills as a basketball player. Just with those one on one games we so competitively played. As I look back it meant a lot to me playing those one on one's with Marshall. Those were some fond memories. As a matter of fact this is what made me the kind of player that I had become in my hoop dream days.

Moreover, as Marshall progressed by his Junior Year in high school, he had become the one player in Carver's history to play every position on the football field. Marshall played kicker, punter, running back, quarterback, cornerback, wide receiver, and maybe once or twice he played center. Marshall was a college scout's dream. Marshall was like a best kept secret, but it became no secret that Marshall was the best thing going. Everybody knew it, he made all American, all purpose player, all everything thing. You name it, Marshall was it. Behind all the accomplishments and achievements and future looking bright, Marshall still had a lot of obstacles to hurdle. He had a lot of personal problems in his life that few knew about.

CHAPTER 5

LOST AND WONDERING WHY

In the midst of all Marshall's achievements and accomplishments he still had a lot of personal hurdles to overcome. No one knew what was beneath the surface. One battle he had to face was the death of his father. His athletic career was taking off, but he was faced with personal battles as well. Marshall became lost and confused, Mr. Roosevelt had died. He had passed away from a terminal disease. He died of cancer. His father's passing left Marshall hurting, feeling alone, lost and in despair. Even though Marshall's dad did not play an active role in his life, they still had a relationship. There still existed a father-son bond. As a friend, I witnessed the highs and lows of Marshall's life. I watched him go through it all.

During this time, Marshall lived with the Bruno's. Living with the Bruno's helped to begin the healing process. He was able to move forward with his life. His mother was experiencing hard times. She could not focus on taking care of her boys. She worked multiple jobs to make ends meet. Ms. Cecile gave her all for her boys. At the time it was just too much to bear. This is one of the reasons why Marshall went to live with the Bruno's in the first place. The Bruno's took Marshall in as one of their own. He became a part of the family. As I mentioned earlier, Mrs. Bruno was an angel in disguise. She was known as Ms. Sibby. Mrs. Bruno was also a single parent, who also struggled with raising two kids of her own. She had hardships as well. Managing to somehow raise her children and living from a meager salary as a cafeteria worker with the Orleans Parish School District. Still she had it in her heart to take in yet another teenager. She graciously took him into her home. This would make it just a little bit harder to make ends meet. She somehow managed to survive. She was a mother to Marshall. This took nothing away from Marshall's mother Ms. Cecile, but she was there at a time of need in Marshall's life. Sometimes in life we need other people and this was one of those times for Marshall and his family. Ms. Sibby was not just a mother figure to Marshall. This was just the way she was with all of his friends. Mrs. Bruno was like a mother to all of her son's friends. That was a quality she possessed. Don't get me wrong she was no push over. Everybody respected her, as a strong black woman. She corrected them when it was necessary. Let's not get it twisted; Ms. Sibby had her struggles like anyone living in a poverty stricken area. That did not stop her from making a way for her children, including Marshall. She welcomed another mouth into her home to feed, shelter and provide for as one of her own. Mrs. Bruno proved that she was truly a blessing in Marshall's life at that time. Through the struggles, ups and downs of life Marshall and Mark developed a bond and became more than just friends. They became brothers. They were inseparable as friends.

CHAPTER 6

THE TRUTH

(Mark and Marshall becomes brothers at Heart)

It's the day of Junior Prom. The day is full of excitement and anticipation because of the prom. The guys attended to their task of the day. This included picking up their tux, rental cars and getting a fresh hair cut. These guys were adamant about getting everything done by noon. Mark and Marshall had a few hours before the prom. The prom was to start at 7:00 pm that evening. In the meantime they had time to get their stunt on. This was a special day to them. They had a chance to drive around in a twenty thousand dollar car. They rented a Dodge Dynasty, a car designed by Chrysler. In those days only people with money or well off had these kinds of cars. Mark and Marshall were just that fortunate; they were able to rent one for that day. They took advantage of it. At that time, coming from where we were from this was a big deal. All that day, Mark and Marshall drove around following each other, showing off for the ladies and anybody in the neighborhood. They acted as if they had purchased the rental cars. After all, these guys were not born with a silver spoon in their mouths.

Mindless Behavior

As they return to the Bruno's house pulling up in the driveway, the boys felt like celebrities. They enjoyed each and every moment of that day. Some of the other fellows showed up to the house to stunt and show off their rental cars as well. It's still early and Mark and Marshall decide to take a ride through the projects and on to the lake front. The guys notice that it is getting close to five pm and they hurry home to get dressed. As time goes by, the guys are finally ready for the prom. This night would be a night that would go down in history. This was the night that Mark and Marshall develop a close bond as friends and brothers at heart.

Its prom night everybody shows up with their dates and looking their best. Mark and Marshall show up and are greeted by everyone. They show up with their dates and these were some fly girls. After all, they are with the most popular guys at the school. These guys were some special guys and they were popular and known by everyone. The prom was held in the hall in Metairie and decorated by the prom committee. There was even a special band there. They were playing songs by Bobby Brown, Keith Sweat and Cameo. This was just to name a few of the kinds of songs that were popular during that time. As prom night progresses and everybody seemed to have a nice time, the night comes to a close. Now the tradition for prom is that everyone is to meet at Denny's after the prom to eat with your date. After that everyone would meet on the Lake Front for an after party. This is where everything would whine down for the night. Some people rented hotel rooms and had parties there.

Tipsy and exhausted from all of the activities of the prom night, Mark and Marshall ended the night in a traditional way. The night was still young for Mark and Marshall, but their dates had to be home for curfew set by their parents. The girls' parents set their curfew for two am. The guys were faithful and had the girl's home by this time. Since they had a nice time at the prom, the guys decided to call it a night. Now this is the defining moment in Marshall's life. Mark noticed that Marshall was a little bit tipsy and suggested that he spend the night. He thought that Marshall would be taking a chance driving intoxicated. He thought about Marshall maybe being stopped by the police, getting into a car accident or any number of things happening to him. Mark again suggested that Marshall spend the night. Since the night of the prom, Marshall would stay at the Bruno home. Despite all of their hardships, the Bruno's welcomed Marshall into their home. Marshall became part of their family.

CHAPTER 7

A MOMENT IN TIME

Now Marshall was always at our home, before he officially moved in with us. He was spending nights here and there and I suggested to my mother that it would be beneficial for Marshall to move in with us. Marshall was having trouble getting to and from practice from across the river. I told my mom that he was here all the time anyway, so it would be a good idea for him to move with us. My mother was apprehensive at first, but she finally agreed and he officially moved in. Now at this time it was Senior Year for the guys. Just to mention, Mark had been playing basketball for Carver and he had become a significant part of the team. He had become sort of a star in his own rite playing as a point guard. Mark was placed on the basketball team in a starting position. He was one of the leading scorers for the team and became the team's captain. Mark also gained recognition in the district as an MVP among some of the best players. Mark had become bound for college and had the potential to become a pro basketball player. Like I said before and I will say it again, sometimes things in life don't always go as planned.

On an average day in the Bruno family home, Mark and Marshall discuss issues that were going on in their lives. They always confided in each other. At the time while living with the Bruno's, Marshall was at the peak of his horizon. Dealing with a tremendous amount of pressure that he faced when deciding which college to attend, Marshall managed to navigate the rites of passage into manhood. He did not have a true father figure that lived with him. He was in need of guidance and advice when it came to making decisions necessary for his life at that time. As a young man, Marshall found it hard to make certain decisions pertaining to the way the world works. He had to figure it out almost on his own. Like most young men without a direct father figure in ones' life. He just did not have enough knowledge about the world he was about to enter. The sports world and how to handle what lie ahead. As a friend, I watched Marshall go through it all. Decisions he made could change his entire life and they did.

While living with us, Marshall had all kinds of college scouts coming to our house and ringing our phone. They all wanted Marshall, he was a hot commodity. Everybody wanted Marshall to play for them. I mean it was unbelievable. They all wanted this meek and humble person who I knew as my friend to play for their school. It was like something out of the movies. They were pulling up in limos and every kind and type of car one could imagine. I mean all the major colleges wanted him. Colleges like LSU, Miami, Nebraska, Connecticut, Notre Dame, and Florida State and so on. If you can name a college, they were probably among those that wanted him. Most of the major colleges wanted Marshall for the position of Defensive Back, but none of them really acknowledged the skills he possessed as a Running Back. Now don't get me wrong, Marshall was just as good as a Corner Back as he was as a Running Back. Marshall was born to run that football. As a friend growing up with Marshall, what I'm about to mention many don't know. I remember him as a young man playing a game we all loved. In the Desire Projects we had this game we played called "Humpty Head". Humpty Head was a creative game we as project kids created. This game, you could say came about because as a kid growing up in poverty you just don't have much. We used our imagination and came up with this game. We would always make up games to pass the time. Humpty Head was just one of those creations. In this game there were four or five opponents playing against each other. Each player would try to make it into an area of the opponents' territory without being touched. If one did get touched, one of his teammates would have to come and free him and make contact with him to release him. Playing this game required certain skills. It was while playing this game that Marshall developed the skills necessary to be a running back. This came about because while playing this game your visual skills were highly developed. You had to be constantly aware of who and where your opponents were. This game also developed Marshall's speed and elusive and evasive qualities. During this game you could not be touched by the opponent, so you had to be fast at eluding your opponent. In order to do this, you had to think fast about which way to turn and escape your opponent. In those days, that game was fun. Marshall was a master at playing this game. When I see Marshall running the ball on any football field,

I imagine him playing Humpty Head. It was there he gained some of the skills that carried him into his greatness as a Running Back. This is where he developed his style as a Running Back, playing the game of Humpty Head.

Moreover, as the pressure of decision making mounted upon Marshall, he became more and more overwhelmed by the whole situation. He was overwhelmed with thoughts of not knowing what to do. He became numb or paralyzed in his decision making. As a friend, I stepped in to try and take some of the heavy load of decision making off of his shoulders. We would discuss some of the decisions that would be best for him. I did not know as much as he knew, but together we looked at different colleges and what they had to offer and came to a decision. I believe that I was instrumental in helping to guide the decision he made for which college he decided to attend. We based the decision on information that was provided to us and based the decision on what he wanted for his life. I just made things a little more apparent and clear for him. It was inside of him all of the time, but he needed a listening ear and someone who understood what he wanted to accomplish. After many trips and visits to college campuses that offered him an athletic scholarship, Marshall still had not made a final decision.

Every trip that Marshall had taken to visit potential colleges, he managed to bring home videos of those colleges. We would sit and review the videos highlighting the benefits of attending some of those schools. Not just for what the school offered in terms of an athletic scholarship, but we also took into account what type of educational programs they had. No matter what Marshall always shared his experiences he had at the schools and always wanted my advice. He always asked my opinion of the school and wanted to know what steps he should take. On one very special day after yet another college visit, Marshall was elated about a visit he had taken to California. Marshall asked Mark to help him unpack as Marshall discussed the details of his visit to California. Mark had never been outside of New Orleans. Marshall: Man it was beautiful out there. The weather was so nice and refreshing. I wish you could have come with me. Mark: Which part of California did you visit? Marshall: San Diego. Mark: Man where can you play college football in San Diego? Did you visit UCLA? Mark did not know much about California. Marshall: Man I visited a school named San Diego State. The name of their team is the San Diego Aztecs. Mark: Man what kind of school is that? Is that some sort of community college? Mark had many questions. Marshall: Man that's a Division 1 School. This school has a nice program. And guess what? This team is the only team that wants me as a running back. You know how long I've wanted play this position. Mark and Marshall ponder the thought of choosing San Diego State based on the idea that this is where Marshall's interests lie. A light goes off in Mark's head. Mark: Man you know I am your friend and I would never steer you wrong. Marshall, I think this would be a good idea for you to accept their offer. Man if I were you, I think I would go and put that school on the map. Now keep in mind San Diego State was not a well known school in the sports world. The school was well known for their graduating rate. They were well known for their educational accomplishments, sports were not mentioned in their repertoire. Mark advises Marshall to attend San Diego State.

Mark predicts that Marshall should go to San Diego State and put the school on the map. Mark felt that if Marshall attended San Diego State, a school unknown in the sports world and bring them the reputation and prestige of having an outstanding football team. By doing so Marshall could bring the attention to the team through his performance. Just as Mark prophesied or had predicted, Marshall signed with the San Diego State Aztecs. Not long after doing so, Marshall took the world by storm. As a friend I witnessed Marshall's journey to success. I was right by his side and watched as the gifts God placed in Marshall unveiled before the world. Marshall became one of the best running backs to ever run a football. It was like we were living in a movie or a dream. If I was to title the movie, it would be titled "The Marshall Faulk Story: His life and Career seen through the Eyes of His Best Friend". Starring Marshall Faulk and co-starring Mark Bruno. That's just how the following events started to unfold before my eyes as his friend. I felt as if my eyes were the lens of a camera and a story was being told. I was living inside of history and I was a part of it. Marshall had a lot of decisions to make, and I was a part of each and every one of those decisions.

Furthermore, Marshall did some amazing things on the field. Some of the accomplishments that he achieved on the football field were unbelievable. I almost could not believe they were real. I had to believe it, because I was there in the stands or on the sideline witnessing these events as they unfolded. If one did not know any better, you'd think I was one of the players, because most of the time I was on the sideline with the rest of the team. That wasn't the case; I was a friend of Marshall who happened to be on the sideline cheering him on. Just because people knew that I was the best friend of Marshall Faulk many people showed me love. Marshall started on a path that would lead him to greatness. In college, I witnessed Marshall break all kinds and types of records. I've witnessed him score touchdown after touchdown. I couldn't believe what Marshall was doing. Once he was unleashed onto the football scene, Marshall exploded as a player. Often times you could hear an entire stadium of people chanting and singing a tune in Marshall's honor. They would often say G-i-v-e . . . . h-i-m . . . . t-h-e . . . . b-a-l-l . . . . Then they would sing Marshall, Marshall, Marshall. The crowd would not stop until they saw him get the ball. Then all you could hear from the stands would be cheering and rumbling in the stands. Now being his best friend and all, I know that Marshall is not a god. Coming from where we come from and witnessing the things that Marshall did on that field was pretty amazing. I would be awaiting him in the parking lot to drive him home and he would get into the car as if nothing had happened after scoring at least five or six touchdowns in one game. Marshall remained humble throughout the whole experience. He did not act as if he was someone great; he just remained the same person I had known all along. Like I stated earlier, this was only the beginning. Through all the success and accomplishments gained by Marshall as a football player he had to face major decisions in his personal life. A demand was constantly being placed on him to go from level to level. He was climbing a ladder. His athletic career was now taking off, but he still faced many obstacles in his personal life. Keep in mind that Marshall is only about nineteen years of age going on twenty. Marshall and I both grew up without male guidance. We did not have a father figure in our lives that would shape and direct our decisions as men. Marshall was the kind of person who had passion for what he was doing, he really did not have the scrutiny or business mind to handle some of the decisions he needed to make. This is the part that I was instrumental in helping him think through and navigate his life's path. Through it all, Marshall and I stuck together and counted sole-heartedly on each other as friends. We confided in each other. I'll never forget the day when Marshall went off to college and left New Orleans to move to California and attend San Diego State. It was the day our lives started down the path of our destiny. Marshall went off to college and I remained in New Orleans. I remained in New Orleans and not going anywhere fast. I was taking life slow. Still cutting hair on my mother's front porch and working a part time job in National Grocery Store. This was a grocery store in our community. Now, I still had dreams of my own and they included going to college, going to the NBA. Thanks to my best friend he somewhat provided a route through which I could also realize my dreams.

CHAPTER 8

LIFE, RESPONSIBILITIES AND RELATIONSHIPS

As Marshall's life progressed and moved forward, he was faced with new situations and realities. He soon discovered that he would be a father. He had no clue of how to deal with this issue. This was a period in Marshall's life that would determine the kind of man he would be. While dating, he had conceived a child with Candace. This was a major change in his life. He had no clue on how to handle this situation. When Marshall met Candace, it was love at first sight. Marshall was not used to dating girls of Candace's stature. She was not only beautiful, but she was intelligent. Candace was majoring in the field of law. She was an aspiring paralegal. To top it off, she was down to earth. When you look at Candace, you would think she was a stuck up type of girl. She was posed and beautiful. She was just the opposite, fun loving and down to earth. Candace was far from the norm, especially in Marshall's eyes. Candace was light brown with a honey complexion. She had beautiful hazel eyes or was they green?

But anyway, Candace took Marshall's heart and ran with it. She had my boy on cloud nine. Marshall was in love.

Moreover, as Marshall and Candace's relationship grew and developed. They became more and more serious. Candace became Marshall's main girlfriend. Candace became a major part of Marshall's life. This was not apparent to everyone. I'll never forget the day when Marshall introduced Candace to the world on national television. It was the ESPY Awards. Candace was Marshall's escort. No one was aware that they were together, at least not in a relationship. It was a shock to everyone. As his best friend, I did not know it was that serious. Well, check this out. This is how everybody found out.

Where can I begin? Back at the campus was where the football team players hung out. I like I said before, it was like I was a member of the team. Marshall's friends were my friends, and most of these guys were on the team. One day we were all in the recreation room, getting ready to watch the ESPY Awards. Everybody wanted to witness Marshall receiving an award. So me and the fellows were all glued to the television cheerful and all in good moods. We were waiting to cheer our buddy on. Now readers, keep in mind what's about to happen a lot of people did not know about. At the time Candace was still involved with a guy she had dated since high school. Candace had moved from Los Angeles with this guy. These two had dated for at least five years. Since attending college, I think their relationship was on shaky ground. They were still involved with each other and somewhat dedicated to each other. Check this out. Let me trip you out. As we sat in suspense to watch the awards in the crowded room of football players, Candace's boyfriend could be spotted in the crowd. We all watched as Marshall made his grand entrance. As the camera focused on Marshall, there was a woman present with Marshall. Everyone wondered who this mystery woman was. As the camera focuses even closer we all discover that this mystery is someone we all knew. It was Candace. Everyone gasped in astonishment. Greg then moves through the crowded room to gain a better view of the television and discovers what we all witnessed. Candace standing at Marshall's side, Gregg then grabs his head and drops to the floor as he exclaims, "that's Candace". No. No. No. The room is in complete silence as we all watched Gregg fall apart. We could not believe it, but we all knew one thing. In the game of life and in the game of love that's the way things are sometimes. You have to roll with the punches. Some might think Marshall was wrong for that. In life and in some situations . . . . Hey! That's how the game goes. Things aren't always fair. Once again Marshall wins. He won his trophy from the ESPY Awards and his trophy woman by his side. From that point on, Marshall Faulk's main lady was Candace.

Likewise, as time goes on their relationship grew rapidly. Marshall had to face another obstacle and a new responsibility. Marshall and Candace conceived their first child. Candace was expecting a baby. All the things that was going on in Marshall's life he was now faced with fatherhood. As I watched my friend graciously transition into fatherhood, it was a privilege to see. Believe it or not I watched my friend transform from a boy to a man. It was nice to see Marshall accept his responsibility as a man and embrace fatherhood the way he did. Knowing that we grew up without a father in our lives, I respected the way he faced this challenge. Now that another star was born, Marshall named his baby boy after himself. He named him Marshall Faulk Jr. He was a spitting image of Marshall. When I say spitting image, I mean literally a spitting image. He was a miniature Marshall. Little Marshall was overwhelming to Marshall Faulk. Keep in mind this was Marshall's first experience of having a kid to call his own. This was major. I as his friend was the closest thing he had to family. I was there to support him as family. You know what? It all worked out. Marshall is now a father, but not quite as happy in his role as being a father. There was so much going on in his life, and this was not something he expected. In addition to it all, Marshall stepped up like a man and took care of his responsibility. Through the process of manhood and fatherhood, Marshall finally accepted his role as being a father and embraced it to the fullest. As time progressed, aka little Deucie became Marshall's bundle of joy. As his friend I was honored to nick name his son Lil Deucie. For some reason Marshall and I idolized the movie "South Central." There was a character in the movie by the name of Lil Deucie. As time progressed Lil Marshall's official nick name was Lil Deucie. He is still known to this day as Lil Deucie, to the ones that know him. His father also had a similar nick name, to the one who knows him best. Marshall's nick name was Dudda. Now, being his best friend for years I never really knew the history of him receiving that nick name. I think his mother gave him that nick name, as to say that's my baby Dudda. To be able to call Mr. Faulk Dudda, you really had to know him. I mean you really had to know him.

Moreover, as Marshall's life transitioned and fell into place Marshall fell deeper and deeper in love with Candace. I can remember

Marshall calling me on the phone one afternoon and asked me what I was doing. I am about to come pick you up, we are going to go roll to a car lot. Now, the first thing that ran to my mind; we're going to the lot to snatch us some rides. At the time Marshall already had a few whips of his own. As he picked me up and we rolled to the dealership, that is the BMW Dealership, I was ecstatic. I was like yeah boy! We are about to do it up. Maybe some matching BMW's with the drop tops. I'm all excited, but I'm not tripping. It wasn't a thing; I already drove most of Marshall's cars like they were mine. That's just how I and my boy were, we shared everything. Any way as we got out of the car, a car salesman greeted us. "Hi Marshall, your car is good and ready", said the salesman. "Wait here, I'm going to the back and pull your car around front." Marshall replies, "ok." As I was pondering the thought, I was in the blind. Marshall never told me anything about what he was about to do. Usually, he shared and confided in me in decisions of this magnitude. For some reason, this time he did not consult with me.

Furthermore, as the salesman drove the car from the back garage, he turned the corner in a clean black top BMW. It was sitting on some chrome Pirellis' twenty two inch rims. They came with the low profile tires. This sucker was clean; you could eat a hot meal off of it. As the salesman rolled up he pulled right in front of us and got out and handed Marshall the keys to a $70,000 dollar car. One of the cleanest I had ever seen at that time. As he conversed with Marshall about the car, at the end of the conversation, I heard the salesman say "I hope your girlfriend Candace likes her car. She's a lucky young lady. For a minute, I thought I was hearing things. That was not the case. Marshall had purchased that $70,000 for Candace. That was the love of his life at that time. It was a huge shock. It literally blew my mind. Even though he was my boy, I did not quite agree or understand how he could make a decision of this magnitude. All in all, whatever made him happy was cool with me. I never questioned Marshall or even asked what made him do that. I had to come to the terms with the fact that my boy was in love. Sometimes love can be blind. We live and we learn, experience is the best teacher.

In addition, to confirm my speculation, Candace's license plate stated, "28 Luvs Me". There it was in bold black print. Wow! Marshall was tripping', he was on cloud nine. I always wondered why the license plate didn't say "I luv 28". That's another story. Well, through it all Candace and Marshall tried to make their relationship last. They went through the ups and downs like any other relationship. They even moved in together as a family, Marshall, Candace and Lil Deucie. Marshall and Candace's relationship lasted a couple of years, some thought it would not last that long. You know what, as Marshall's friend watching Marshall go through this situation, it might have worked. If it had not been for the strain placed on their relationship of Marshall's rise to fame and success, they might just have made it. To tell you the truth I don't care what anyone says, I know Marshall and Candace may have still been together. They probably would have been happily married and with more kids. But, they were young and did not know how to balance their relationship. That's life, we live and we learn. Nowadays, Marshall and Candace are the best of friends. They are dedicated parents to their son, Marshall Faulk Jr. Candace has moved on with her life and married Derrick Fisher of the Los Angeles Lakers. Derrick Fisher is known for being an elite point guard in the NBA and went on to win five championships for the Los Angeles Lakers. Candace and Derrick Fisher had a daughter together. Marshall went on to marry Lindsay Stoudt whom he fathered three daughters with. Marshall also conceived a son with a woman by the name of Helen Dunn a fitness trainer.

Furthermore, Marshall and Candace couldn't maintain the relationship. They ended a relationship that could have worked out for the better. I as his friend witnessed my buddy go through multiple relationships after the relationship with Candace ended. Marshall was on a mission to find the right one. As a friend of both Marshall and Candace, and knowing them personally a part of me wanted to see them stay together. That's just my opinion.

CHAPTER 9

THE SIGNIFICANT ONES

Through it all, college and the ups and the downs, the trials and tribulations Marshall had a lot of people in his life that still cared for him like family. There was this guy by the name of Curtis Johnson. He recruited Marshall from Carver to journey to San Diego State to become an Aztec. When I first met Mr. Johnson better known as C.J., he was not like the average recruiter. He did not try to bait me in, in order to get close to Marshall. C.J. was a cool brother real down to earth. He had a very positive energy about himself. He gave off the energy, of having a vibe as a down to earth and real person. He gave you the feeling that he had your best interest at heart. C.J. would come by the house on the weekends to check on us or to see if we wanted to shoot hoops or something. C.J. didn't just wear the recruiter's hat; he came off more like a friend to us. Even though he wanted Marshall to desperately sign with San Diego State; He didn't handle Marshall like signing was the only thing that mattered. C.J. had Marshall's best interest at heart. As Marshall's best friend and other pair of eyes, I recognized and convinced Marshall that C.J.

was a good dude. C.J. was one of San Diego States' best recruiters. He helped to bring all kinds of great athletes to San Diego State University. He was a magnet to potential stars. Instead of him being a recruiter and a coach, he probably missed his calling as an agent. But that's just my opinion. C.J. could have been a well known agent with a legacy of well known athletes he molded and inspired. Now that I look back, I'm glad C.J. was a part of our lives. Nowadays, C.J. is coaching for the New Orleans Saints. He has moved on to accept a position as the Head Coach for Tulane University's Green Wave. He deserves the recognition that he is now receiving as one of the best coaches there are. Curtis Johnson a man of integrity and honor and a true friend indeed. I will never forget another person that Marshall and I were fortunate to cross paths with in life. That person was none other than C.J.'s dad. Mr. Curtis Johnson Sr. played the role as a father figure and mentor to Marshall and me. Mr. Johnson Sr. was a City Council Member for the city of St. Rose, Louisiana. He fought for justice and righteousness on the behalf of the people of St. Rose, Louisiana. Mr. Johnson Sr. accepted Marshall and me into his home and as one of his own. The relationship stemmed from the relationship that we had with C.J. When we were all together it felt like family. The love we had for one another was genuine. I can attest to the fact that the Lord puts people in your life for a reason. The reason C.J. and his father was a part of our lives can be simply stated as direction. Later on down the years, Mr. Johnson Sr. passed away. He will be missed but not forgotten. Thank God for people like that. May Mr. Johnson rest in peace and know that the work he did was not in vain. He touched lives. For that reason, he will always be remembered.

On the other hand, the relationship that Marshall and I had with C.J. and his father, I can't say about everybody. You know there were people who wanted to get close to Marshall. They wanted a piece of the pie. There was this guy that almost pops up out of nowhere. He became one of the most significant people in Marshall's life. He remains a significant part of Marshall's life to this day. This is none other than Rocky Arceneaux. Let me tell y'all about this cat. Rocky was a friend of C.J. C.J. introduced us to this guy. He is an agent. Now, an agents' job is to represent and manage players. Agents negotiate contracts and make deals on the behalf of the athletes they represent. Unlike C.J. he was not the guy that was down to earth. He was about his business. His business was to get Marshall's career on the right path and to get Marshall to sign with his company. He came with his guns loaded. Rocky was unknown, but he was in the game for a while. So this means that he had the experience and knowledge we lacked about the business aspect of an athletic career. He knew all of the moves, all the right people and plays to make. He needed a client. He needed somebody big. Marshall was that big fish of an athlete, that could make or break his career as an agent. I'm not taking anything from Rocky or his character. To be in this business, one needs heart. Heart he had. When I first met Rocky through C.J. and Marshall, I didn't pay Rocky too much mind. I didn't take the time to be judgmental about him. Rocky was always on the move. He was always popping up at events or always calling and checking on us. He even invited us to a party or an event or something. At the time I knew nothing about sports agents or anything to do with the business side of sports. All I knew was a thing or two about playing in the game of sports. Other than that I didn't know anything about a sports agent or representative or whatever you want to call it. As I grew to know Rocky he began to grow on all of us. We accepted him as friend. Just like all the others, Rocky became more like family than just a friend. Rocky was the oldest member of our circle. Rocky was very experienced in the business. Before he met Marshall he was experienced and established as an agent in the sports world. He had clients and business partners that kept his name well known to the sports business world. The day he met Marshall Faulk, he would not have known that his life was about to change so drastically. Through it all Rocky was consistent with developing Marshall's Career. Journey with me as I reflect on the friendships that were shared between, Rocky, Marshall and me (Mark Bruno).

Reflecting back on our Friendship
(Marshall, Rocky, and Mark)

As Marshall's Career progressed, Marshall's circle of friends grew larger. People were coming from everywhere and wanted to be friends with Marshall. Everyone wanted to be a part of Marshall's success. As Marshall's childhood friend and now his best friend as adults, I never looked at Marshall the way others did. To me Marshall was the same guy. Except now he had an extraordinary career. This was the person I shared life's ups and downs with and everyday struggles. I can honestly say that Marshall was the same person I knew growing up. Others saw Marshall and they were simply star struck. People were being nice to me just because I was Marshall's best friend. On the other hand, I never had an experience that could be compared to what Marshall was experiencing in his career. He had reached a level of success in his career and as I walked with him through this period in his life, I met with all kinds of people. There were people who wanted to be close to Marshall to fulfill their own agendas. Some of these people were snakes in the grass, plotting, strategizing, showing jealousy and enviousness and just being devils in disguise. They were coming out of the blue as well. Marshall had a lot to face. There were a lot of smiling faces that did not have Marshall's best at heart. They wanted to get close to him to achieve their personal goals. Well, like the saying goes we live and learn and experience is the best teacher. What I learned and experienced through that period of time all the things I've mentioned above about the characteristics of some people; this was the major cause of the turbulence that played a part in destroying the friendship that Marshall and I had. At that level of success, money and fame, you better know who your friends are. I'm here to let you know from my experience a lot of things can get twisted. That's another story. Through it all believe it or not, Marshall, me and Rocky kept a tight knit friendship within the circle. We all remained close friends. Within our relationship there were roles that we played in Marshall's life. I was his best friend, confidant, right hand man, main source etc. Rocky was a native of New Orleans, so he understood a lot about our culture. He was cool dude and he was a potential business partner for Marshall. He tried his best to demonstrate that he was the best man for the job and that he did. We not only had a professional relationship, we had a personal relationship and we all grew closer. We all did a lot of things together. To name a few we partied, went to concerts, business ventures, and met high profile people, you name it we did it. You know what, we lived the life and we shared a lot of significant moments.

Meeting the Owner of the Colts

Moreover, Marshall, Rocky and I spent a lot of significant moments and leisure time together. But this day, this is a day that I will never forget. I, Rocky, and Marshall went to meet with the owner of the Colts team. The Owner of the Indianapolis, Colts wanted to make a deal with Marshall. They wanted Marshall to sign. It was a day that was surreal to me. I can only imagine how it was for Marshall. Well, why should I imagine? I was there. Just imagine two kids coming from the poverty stricken streets of New Orleans Ninth Ward, sitting in a round table discussion with billionaires discussing a Multi-Million Dollar Contract. Not only that, but imagine my friend who I played "Humpty-Head" in the Projects as their main interest during the discussion. This discussion has to do with my friend entering a life of riches, fame and to top it off the NFL. This is what we had dreamed of as boys on those rough streets of the Desire Project. It was finally happening. Can you just imagine going from rags to riches? I hate to say it, but this is another one of those stories. It pays to dream big. We dreamed big, and that big dream happened. Can you imagine that feeling? Well I did. I lived it. It is a feeling and a moment that I will treasure forever.

In addition to what I was feeling, let me tell you more details about that day. As we pulled up in to the Colts facility a phone call came through on the car phone. It was the Colt's owner wanting to know if we were on schedule for the meeting. The White Lincoln Continental Limousine, pulled up to the Colts facility and we were greeted by the business owners of the Colts. Audience, believe it or not I was not enthusiastic about the team, because I am a New Orleans Saints fan. Once inside the meeting room, Rocky began the introductions. Once we were all seated the negotiations began. Man, once inside this state of the art facility and seeing the grounds where the Colts practice this experience was unbelievable. Even though I was seated at the table and feeling all the objects around me, this experience was still unreal to me. It took me a while to get a grip on what was taking place. Once I gained my composure and realized it's really happening, I pulled Marshall aside. I just wanted to talk to him to see what he was thinking and to ask if he had made any decisions. This was big and it was happening. What was happening; was not about the money. It was about a dream come true. We were about 21 years of age and some people in their 40's won't ever experience what we experienced on that day. We were age of majority, but we were really still kids. This was beyond our wildest dreams. We didn't even grasp the whole event until it was all over.

The Colts Owners and business associates begin to make small talk with us. I guess this was to ease the tension we were feeling, but they were feeling it in a different way. These guys had Marshall and they wanted him. As bad as we wanted this dream, was how equally bad they wanted Marshall to sign for the team. There was some tension in that room, and it wasn't just coming from me and Marshall. I'll never forget the conversation we had with each other as well as the small talk that was exchanged in that room on that day. Man the first thing that came out of my mouth is I wish Coach Reese was here. This man was a mentor to us and he would not steer us wrong and he kept a level head. We had no one, but ourselves to make this decision and hope that it is the right one. We were nervous and indecisive. Marshall knew he wanted to play ball, but he had not given the business side of the game any thought. Man we looked at each other eye to eye; held our heads up and stuck our chest out. We looked at each other and said in unison, "Man it's going down." We gave each other some dap and said it's finally here. Deep down inside we had the feeling inside that said "man up dog, this is the time and it's the season." My friend had made it to the pros and I was there witnessing the whole event as his life would change forever. We rejoined the meeting and negotiations began. The business owners were still making small talk. The small talk stopped and they all became intensely serious and the negotiations began. The Colts owner, Mr. Robert Irsay looked around the room and spoke of how it was his pleasure to have acquired this meeting time with Marshall. As the meeting was about to begin we all stepped into the meeting room and everybody sat down. We were seated at a round table, we were all ready to discuss the business of the day. The business of the day was primarily to get Marshall as a team member for the Colts. Mr. Irsay was the owner of the Colts and it was a pleasure for me to meet him. I had never met anyone of his stature. Mr. Irsay briefly introduced himself and took his seat at the head of the table.

During this time Mr. Irsay began discussing what he wanted to offer Marshall if he would agree to sign with his team. As I recall that day, I remember Mr. Irsay being straight forward, direct, to the point and strictly about business. To tell you the truth, even though Marshall and I were from the ghetto, these are the kind of people we were accustomed to dealing with. Meaning most people we knew was about their business and didn't have time for anything other than business. From this aspect and talking with Mr. Irsay we sort of had a good connection and he seemed to want that connection with us. You could see that he made the people he did business with feel comfortable before just going for the kill. He took his time and let you know what kind of a person you were doing business with.

It's time for business and being Marshall's Agent Rocky stepped up and took charge of the situation. He went into action and did what he does best. He began the negotiations and worked out the deal in Marshall's favor. So as Rocky began to take charge and work out the specifics of the contract, so many things began to go through my mind. I was still caught up in the moment and so was Marshall. Honestly, Marshall always kept a humble attitude and was good at keeping his composure in tough situations. Me on the other hand could have jumped out of my skin because of all of the excitement. Keep in mind, Marshall was the hottest thing coming out of college and entering the draft. Marshall was considered a lottery pick. This meant that he was among the top three draft picks. This usually meant that you would automatically become an instant millionaire or franchise player. Let's get back to the meeting. Rocky finished negotiating the deal. He had negotiated to the best of his ability at what he felt was one of the best deals he could get for Marshall and Mr. Irsay. They finally came up with some numbers and an offer placed on the table. Rocky stopped the meeting for intermission and to consult with me and Marshall. Rocky met with us in a room outside of the meeting room apart from everybody else. He sat us down and began to give us the highlights of the negotiations he had agreed upon with Mr. Irsay. As Rocky began to speak he said you know I Love you guys like brothers. What I'm about to tell you about Mr. Irsay wants to offer you is truly a blessing from God. Marshall! Mr. Irsay wants to offer you a 2.2 million dollar contract and a signing bonus for 11 million, if you will agree to play for him for seven years as his franchise player. I never saw Marshall lose his composure, but when Rocky told us that, Marshall broke down with tears of joy. Rocky, Marshall and I shared a bond and in that moment, this bond grew stronger. My boy had made it to the Pro's. Marshall and I jumped up and down with excitement, but we soon regained our composure.

As we returned to the meeting; the whole group of business associates was awaiting our decision. We all took our seats, Marshall stood to announce that he had decided to accept the offer from the colts and sign the contract. The atmosphere in the room was filled with the anticipation they had so long awaited. Marshall and I could feel the presence of God as he gave his final answer. This was a dream come true. Before Marshall could sign on the dotted line, Mr. Irsay stood to say a few words. Mr. Irsay asked Marshall a few questions to confirm and gain assurance that Marshall understood what was being expected of him. He wanted to know if Marshall understood and knew for sure if this was something he wanted to embark upon. Mr. Irsay stood and began to question Marshall. Mr. Irsay: Marshall I need to know from you, if you can give me a thousand yards rushing every season? Can you give me at least five hundred yards receiving a season? Marshall, I want to know can you give your all towards being a member of my team and organization. Marshall stood and looked up at Mr. Irsay and looked directly into his eyes. Marshall shook Mr. Irsay's hand and stated, "I promise you that and more." After hearing Marshall's response, Mr. Irsay smiled as he looked at Marshall and then looking around the room, he chuckled. Mr. Irsay then chuckled once more and said, "I like this guy, good answer." Mr. Irsay handed Marshall the pen and said, "sign here, young man." "Glad to have you." It was times like these that went down in history. That was just one moment of many fond memories to come. The list goes on and on.

Fond Memories

I can remember moments so vividly it's as if they were yesterday.

1. Accompanied Marshall for Draft Day in New York.
2. Accompanied Marshall to the Heisman Event.
3. Marshall, Rocky and I met Janet Jackson for one of her concerts in person. Believe it or not she thought that I was kind of cute and wanted to accompany me for a photo. (Indianapolis Concert)
4. Marshall's first autograph signing as a rookie. Marshall signed 250 rookie cards with my assistance.

5. Living with Marshall in a mansion he purchased in Indianapolis.

6. Appeared in a commercial with Marshall in San Diego. This commercial was made in the school's library the commercial was made to encourage kids to read more.

7. Always on the sideline for Marshall's College games.

8. I can remember being best friend, personal assistant, confidant and right hand man.

9. Those were some good times and experiences, but in life I've learned that things change and people change. Now I want to share some life experiences that were pertaining to my life. My fall from grace.

CHAPTER 10

MY FALL FROM GRACE

Marshall and I had been friends most of our lives. We have been through it all; we were true friends until the end. At least that is what I believed. I thought we would be friends until the end. This is the beginning, the apex, and the height of our relationship and I could not figure out where things began to go wrong. As I think about the day Marshall and I parted ways, there are things I still didn't understand.

It has been many years since Marshall and I have been close friends and I'm a mature person. There are some things that I finally can understand. It took maturity and life experiences to help me to understand the things I once could not. It has been nothing but the grace of God that brought me this far in my life. He has helped me see what my divine purpose in life is. The friendship that I shared with Marshall was unlike any friendship that I have had in my life. Part of that was based on our path in life to find ourselves as men. As I reflect on my younger years, I can see that the role I played in Marshall's life and his role in mine was none other than to fulfill a divine purpose. I was not just some person taking a ride in someone else's life; I had a specific part to play. He directly and indirectly helped me discover the potential I had inside. I directly and indirectly helped him to reach and achieve his goals. It's a trip how important to him I was as a friend and vice versa.

As Marshall's life and career began to grow, so did he. He began to mature as a man and he began to transition into the man he was supposed to be. I as his best friend could not understand it all at the time. I could not understand the changes he was making at that time. Marshall was changing and transitioning right in front of me. His life, relationships and our friendship was taking on changes. I just could not understand where it was all leading to. It was overwhelming and unbearable for me. Marshall's success was something he had to brace himself for and I as his friend found myself being left out of parts of his life. He would consult me about almost everything. He no longer saw me as his equal. He now expected me to play a role that was less than what I had been all along, his friend. I took all of these changes personal. At that time it felt as if, it was a direct insult to me as a man. I either had to embrace the change, for whatever it was or I had to leave it all behind. Through it all, the journey to his success, and fame, I never thought Marshall and I would be distant friends. We would become as if we were strangers and had never known each other. Some people might believe that this is messed up, or even say that's a shame. For those who knew the history behind our relationship probably have a hard time believing what I am now revealing. People probably feel like Marshall changed on me. People probably still think that we have a close relationship, but I am here to say that they are wrong. We no longer have a close bond like brothers. Well readers, I want to give you insight on the real situation. As I grew in maturity, I realized that I can't fault Marshall. I now look at things from a different perspective, as a mature adult.

Moreover, for a long period of time, I was angry at Marshall. I felt like he was angry at me and that he had turned his back on me. He was changing and he acted as if he did not even know me. He acted as if he and I had never been close friends. This drove me crazy and I was lost and confused, frustrated and mad. I just could not understand why things had turned for the worst. I had always been a true friend to Marshall. Why was this happening and why was it happening now. So I went through this personal turbulence and struggle in my mind. I thought about it over and over and could not understand what I had done wrong. Why has he changed, was he ashamed of me. Was he ashamed of his roots, now that his environment and the people around him now changed? Where I had once belonged, he made me feel as if I no longer belonged. Why is he forgetting where we came from? Or did he want to forget that part of his life? All of these questions and doubts about our past friendship surfaced in my mind. All these elements played a part in my fall from grace. My fall was not just my departure from his life, but it was what I did next. I had entered a dark period of my life. This place is so dark that many don't make it out to tell their story. Thanks to my Lord and Almighty Savior, I have. It wasn't easy as I reflect back on my living in this dark period. I was living in the shadow of someone else's life. No one saw me, everyone saw Marshall when they looked at me. They did not know the personal hell that I was going through. People thought because I was Marshall's friend, I had it all. I was just going through the motions of living life. My life was passing me by. I was stuck; it was like I was spell bound. I could not get passed it and I was stuck in this dark period of my life. I had to pick up the pieces to my life and I could not. I did not know where to begin. I was going through a kind of depression, the kind that people go through when you lose some one through death. I was grief stricken. I was losing hope for my life every day. Instead of turning to God, I then turned to drugs. I had made the biggest mistake of my life. I wanted the pain to stop and drugs were the only way I knew how.

Through all the pain, hurt and rejection the problem grew worst. I used drugs to numb my feelings of pain and to block out the everyday realities. The person that I thought I knew and the person I thought knew more about me than I knew about myself did not give a damn about me. Here I was lost, confused, mad with the world, mad with myself and mad at Marshall. I was going through a personal storm. In my mind was nothing but turbulence. I felt like a volcano had erupted inside of me. My life was spiraling out of control. I had forgotten how to chase my dreams. I had lost purpose for my life. I did not know how to go and pick up the pieces and fragments that were left behind. I had lost who I once was. Where had my basketball career gone and my college days. Where had it all gone. The friends, the cars, the money, the girls where was it all, where were they? I landed myself in and out of jail. Who could have ever imagined it? Mark Bruno, Marshall Faulk's best friend in and out of jail. Me, myself I could not even believe it. I had become a slave and in bondage to a habit. I knew this is not what my mother had raised me to be or who God had intended for my life. It all had gone wrong.

Furthermore, I still had this stigma hanging over my head. I was no longer Mark Bruno, people saw me only as Marshall Faulk's best friend. At least the people that knew me and who knew the history of my connection to Marshall. I was stuck in this shadow and it overshadowed the person that I was. There was so much more to me than just being someone's friend. People did not see that. Living with that stigma attached to me and the shadow that was cast over my life people treated me different. People thought that just because I was Marshall's friend, that I had it made. Believe it or not, everyone was not happy about Marshall's success. I was the person who was left to face these people. They were haters, jealous and upset at the fact that Marshall had made it out and they did not. Some people felt like I deserved to be back at ground zero. They wanted to see me suffer because of having the opportunity to know what it was to make it out and have to return to the realities of what they were living. I was in between two walls. One wall was not being fully accepted by friends and neighbors in a community, where I was raised and born. Another wall was the rejection from a life-long friend who had totally turned his back on me. Where would I go from here? The wall of rejection from my friend cast a shadow over my life from which I thought I would not escape. Many people just did not get it. They did not know the personal storm that I had to confront.

If they had known the truth, they really would not want to believe it. I had nothing and I mean I literally nothing. I had to pick up and start over again. I had to build a new life for myself and realize regardless of the mistakes that I made I needed to make a change. I had to bring my life to Christ to straighten it all out. I had been leaning on my own understanding. I had decided to lean on him for guidance; my Lord and Savior Jesus Christ. This is when my life started to change and took on meaning again. I had been counted out, left for dead, finished silenced forever, and never to resurface again. The burning inside me concerning my life and the life I had once lived would not die. God was pulling me closer to him and trying to get my attention.

Furthermore, my transformation into the person I am today was not an easy one. I had not completely surrendered to the direction God wanted me to take in my life. I still had a lot of anger inside of me relating to the issue that I had with Marshall. As my relationship to God grew stronger he began to guide me. He spoke to me and told me that I needed to let the anger go. This was something that had derailed my life, but it was not the end of my life. God related to me that the greatest part of my life was in front of me and not behind me. He told me that I had to stop living my life based on what had happened in my past and what I thought was supposed to have happened. He had greater things in store for me. I am God. If I say something is going to happen or allow it to happen, it will only be so if I say so. I am God and I wrote the book of life. It was at that very moment that a heavy burden was lifted from my shoulders. I started to think differently. My conscious became clearer and I knew within myself I had to change the way I was living and the way I was going about my life. I decided that I did not need drugs in my life. The recovery process started to take place. I felt like I could finally make it. I decided that I would take the negatives and turn them around for the positive. After all, my relationship to Marshall was not my whole life, it was just a part of my life. I had things inside of me that needed to be cultivated. I now thank God for allowing me to have the experiences that I had while I was a close friend of Marshall. That chapter of my life is over. I can honestly say that I thank God and I thank Marshall for that period in my life. I thank God because he allowed me to go through the trials and the tribulations so that I can find the person who I am. I also thank Marshall, because if he had not rejected me I would not have found the man inside of me that needed to be seen by the world. I had to find me. The rejection helped me to find me and helped me to continue to follow my dreams.

In addition, if you think about it I would have still been doing the same things I did when I was young. Since my exit from Marshall's life, I found the man that God intended for me to be. If Marshall had not rejected me, I would have remained inside of a shadow. Now, I am following my dreams and the purpose that God had intended for my life. My perspective now is that I realize with a strong passion that everything happens for a reason. Although everybody's situation is different, I believe all things happen for a reason.

This brings me to the subject of reason. The dictionary defines reason as that of which is in accordance and ratified by the mind rightly exercised having the right intellectual judgment; clear and fair deductions from true principals; that which is dictated or supported by the common sense of mankind; right conduct; right propriety and most of all justice(Merriam and Webster, 2011). I realize now that God allowed me to go through all I have went through to build in me endurance, knowledge and wisdom. With this knowledge and understanding he has placed in me I can help someone else through those experiences. He also has given me strength, courage, knowledge, wisdom, self discovery, love for myself, a conquering spirit, and the most gratifying one of them all is the soul-survivor in me. My new heart and mind has forgiven Marshall.

I had to stop thinking of only myself and place myself in Marshall's shoes. I had to empathize with him. I had to realize that the world does not revolve around me. I am a vessel in the hands of God, and made for his use. Now don't get that twisted and think that I am on some ego trip. Everybody has the ability to be used by him. Through my self-examination I realized that Marshall was living out his call on his life. He was created to go where he went and was fulfilling what God had intended for his life. He was doing what he had to do to fulfill his God given destiny. He had to make the necessary changes to his life in order to accomplish the things he had to accomplish in his life. The changes he made to his life were not directed at me and it was not a personal attack on me. He made the changes that were needed to complete his mission. He had to become excellent in all the he said and did to excel where he was. This was not personal. I had rebelled against the necessary changes, but my friend had embraced the necessary changes that needed to be made. I had a destiny to fulfill as well. I had things to conquer and overcome. I had to really dig deep and find the reasons within myself and figure out why.

Now as I have matured I now understand the reasons why. I challenge anyone who is reading this book to stop and reflect on your life. Take an evaluation of yourself and dig deep inside. Don't look at the negative circumstances that surround your situation and look deeper. It may seem hurtful, it might seem as if no one cares, it may even seem as if there is no way to overcome. I want you to know that there is a reason behind everything that happens in life, the good and the bad. Remember to look at the situation as God see's it. It all is for the plan that God has for your life.

My Shared Reasons

1. It was a reason Marshall and I was childhood friends.
2. It was a reason my mother allowed Marshall to live in our home just as one of her own children.
3. It was a reason I experienced all that I experienced with Marshall.
4. It was a reason I was there to help Marshall make intricate decisions concerning his life.
5. It was a reason I experienced a period of rejection by Marshall and others.
6. It was a reason Marshall changed.
7. It was a reason I experienced a fall from grace.
8. It was a reason I experienced the lowest low of my life going to and fro from jail.
9. It was a divine reason I surrendered my life to Christ.
10. It was a reason to recognize God's calling on my life.

11. It was a reason God gave me the strength to endure the writing of this book.

12. There is a reason that this book had to be written.

Spiritual Awakening

The reasons that were mentioned earlier are just a testament to how my life turned around and this book can help others realize in themselves through self reflection the reasons that events occurred in their lives. There are things in life that must be fulfilled. There is just no way to avoid it, it has to happen. When those things happen it is only a vehicle that gets you to that next level in your life you must face and overcome. Since finding the Lord and surrendering to him my eyes have been opened to the truth about my life. The blind folds have been removed from my eyes. It is a trip how one significant relationship in a person's life defines a meaning and purposes in another person's life. This is kind of impossible to recognize without having a personal relationship with God and understanding how he works. The things I experienced I would not want my worst enemy to go through. I know you readers are probably thinking, damn was this situation that serious? Yes, I as a living and walking testimony would not want my worst enemy to have walked in my shoes. I had to come face to face with adversity; I was dealing with this situation of living in the shadow. I have come to the conclusion that I do not have any regrets. After all, I've learned a lot from going through this journey. Like the old saying goes, only if I would have known what

I know now. You know what? That's life! We go through things and sometimes have to face tough situations.

If I had the chance to rewind it all, I don't think I would change a thing. I'm a strong believer in the fact that, a person has to go through what he or she has to go through to develop into the person they are going to become. Look at me. I'm here to tell and share my story, to uplift, to inspire, to bring awareness and truth about how I overcame adversity.

Moreover, I strongly believe that there's going to be a day in everybody's life that there is going to be some kind of adversity. I wrote this book in hopes that someone could be helped from my story and to help them face that mountain of adversity. I hope m y experiences I shared in this book would be that extra boost that someone may need to make it over that mountain and help them make it to the other side. I hope that this book helps people to make it to the other side where there is abundant life and a guiding light that lies within us all. Therefore, I wrote this book as a testament of my experiences. It is not just a book about the time I spent as a friend of Marshall and being his best friend of someone of his stature. This book is about self discovery and finding myself; after being caught up in someone else's dream. Through it all, I had to find self worth. This is something I share with you the reader in my next chapter of Self Discovery.

CHAPTER 11

SELF DISCOVERY

My experience with finding myself was no easy task. I had to come to a point in my life where I had to judge myself and look deep into my inner self to find who I really was. Finding oneself takes a lot of good and bad experiences. For some it can take a life time, for some it may be a situation. It can be as instant as a blink of an eye. It all depends on the person and life experiences that one might encounter. In my case, I had to get dragged through mud. I had to fall from grace. I had to hit rock bottom to see and reflect within myself. I had to come to the conclusion that there was a better me inside and still alive waiting and kicking. Throughout my life as I reflect on myself back then, I was always the type of person with a good character. I've always had a good reputation, I've perceived that people enjoyed being around me. Once I was caught up in Marshall's life and being a true and loyal friend to him. Somehow I lost myself and my life took a 360 degree change. I was dropped from his life. Out of nowhere, I did not know who to blame. It was like I was dropped out of the sky into the Pacific Ocean without a boat, life jacket or a paddle. I feel like I was dropped and someone saying, now make it to shore. This is just how I perceived it. Now imagine that. This situation was either going to make or break me. That's when the inner me rose and stood up. All that I was and who I am today had come full circle. Who I was had been forced to the surface. I had to realize my true value within. A part of me had to be discovered to continue my journey and divine purpose to reach my destiny. God had a plan for me. Discovering my inner me, I had to realize God's specific plan was for me to experience and endure all that I had gone through. I was being prepared for where God was taking me. Once I discovered that and analyzing the different situations that I went through, I could better understand that it was all a part of God's plan. I dug deep down within myself and guess what? I found and discovered that I had no clue of what was hidden inside me. I realized that I had hidden treasure within myself. I had a new sense of self worth. I found that I had the ability to tell a story. I had a story within myself. I found the author inside of Mark Bruno. I knew that there was a book inside of me was the book of my life.

Once I began writing, I knew that this was the call on my life. There was a new direction I had taken. It created a kind of peace within me. I could tell a story about my life, from my perspective. I found a voice where there once was no voice about what had happened in my life. Discovering that, everything fell into place. Everything started to make sense. Everything that I had been through, started to line up with destiny.

Destiny

What I've discovered about destiny is that, it is the apex one's life. The word destiny can be defined as a final outcome, independent of the events that precede, which are inevitable and unchangeable per themselves, but as a sequence that could be arranged and rearranged in order to arrive to the final outcome. There is the often confusing argument that individuals can choose their own destiny by selecting different "paths" throughout their lives, even though the different courses of action the individuals take none the less lead to a very predetermined destiny. To escape the contradiction, the incompatibility of philosophical terminology of this argument and fully support the concept of destiny most believe it necessary to declare and accept this notion of choice (freewill) as an illusion. We have to understand that, and come to believe that freewill and destiny can coincide in harmony. Simply, "DESTINY HAS BEEN ENVISAGED AS FORE-ORDAINED BY THE DIVINE, A HIGHER CALLING WE ALL ARE DESTINED TO REACH" (Merriam Webster Dictionary, 2010). Discovering my true value and worth, I no longer feel like the victim of my circumstances, but feel more now like the victorious one through my perseverance. Now I know that everything that I have been through was ordained by God. I had to go through what I went through in order to reach my destiny. I never thought my faith and life's ultimate test would come in a form of adversity. Moreover, that it would come through a broken friendship. I was challenged through my experiences and through the journey that I traveled as being the best friend of Marshall Faulk.

CHAPTER 12

THROUGH TRIALS AND TRIBULATIONS

There is always a Bright Side of the Darkness

Now, I see myself as a victor. When I look back, I now know that there is a bright side of things. One must open their minds and develop a sense that there is always a bright side to negative situations. The bright side of my situation is that I discovered myself. I found out things that I would not have otherwise known if I had not gone through the pain, the hurt, and the rejection that I had to face throughout my fall from grace. I would have not gotten to meet the better side of me, that strong man on the inside of me. I would have never gained the knowledge and wisdom that I have now that helps me better able to face any situation. I used to hear people say, look at the bright side. I use to hear people say that, but I never knew what it meant to really try and find something positive about a negative situation. Now I do have the insight necessary to see a bright side to any situation and knowing that there is always a bright side. Experience is the best teacher. Like the late Betty Wright says in a song entitled, "no pain, no gain." I learned the hard way; that this theory of how to look at life situations is can sometimes hold true.

Learning from life's hard situations is a great feeling. Knowing that you have a priceless possession on the inside that's worth more than any amount of money is a wonderful realization. This brings me to the definition of knowledge. According to Merriam Webster, knowledge is the state or fact of knowing familiarity, awareness or understanding gained through experience or study(Webster, 2010). Webster also states that the sum or range of what has been perceived, discovered or learned is knowledge. It's also the specific information about something, it's carnal knowledge. These are all defined as knowledge. So this implies that knowledge is based on one's experiences. From those experiences we gain knowledge. Our knowledge is solely based on what we experienced and learned through direct observation of a happening or event.

I now have the knowledge that I lacked back then. In the past Marshall and I were just young men, in the midst of a world that we were strangers to. We had no knowledge of this world and we were thrown into it. This world included money fame, success, celebrities. With all of those aspects of this world comes, deceit and uncertainty. Everybody you encounter almost use what you don't know against you. Because we lacked knowledge we were taken by storm and our friendship was twisted in its midst. It was like we had been hit by a whirlwind and we were in a tornado. We had to adjust to this new world and we had to do it almost instantly. Like I say in my story, in life some things have to happen. They are inevitable, but necessary.

Through it all, I've also learned that life is like a big puzzle connected with pieces that are put together to display a representation. In order for the puzzle to be complete, it has to have all of the pieces in the right places in order for it to display the right image. If all of the pieces are in their right place they show the full picture and its meaning. Through it all, I still believe that I was a divine piece of the puzzle of my friend's life. That part of my life was significant and it shaped and molded me into who I am today. My life and the pieces of the puzzle from that chapter are finally complete, they have been connected. There may be a piece here and there that is still missing. In time these will be connected as well. As I look back, I know the pieces fit and are coming together, because here I am writing a book and sharing my experiences and knowledge with the world. Looking at the bright side of it all, it was all part of a divine plan.

I will never forget the time I was locked up in prison. This was the time Marshall's team went to the Super Bowl, 2000. I was not there. This was the first time out of many times that Marshall and I were not together. I was incarcerated. This was truly an event that proved to me how important my friendship with Marshall was. After breaking several records and scoring a few touchdowns in his first Super Bowl appearance; Marshall's team won the Super Bowl. While being interviewed at the end of the game, Marshall was asked about how he felt after all that he had accomplished that night. I'll never forget Marshall saying, that he was grateful and thankful to have achieved what he had done. On national television he stopped and looked straight into the camera, "what would put the icing on the cake if my best friend Mark Bruno would have been here to share in this moment with me." "Mark Bruno man, keep your head up." As I stood in front of the television along with the other inmates, I was shocked and could not believe he would even make an appeal like that on television. At that moment I knew that my friendship had some impact on Marshall. Every one turned and looked at me and could not believe that I was actually telling the truth about being the best friend of Marshall Faulk. I feel that it is necessary for me to share some of the bright side of my story with the readers. I don't want my story to come off as if Marshall was the villain. I might not have agreed with the way he handled certain things in this situation, he has never been the bad guy. Now that I look at it and see how far my friend has come, I could do nothing but be proud of him. I know that my family was a part of the history of why Marshall is successful. We were a blessing to him. We were instrumental in helping Marshall get to where he is today. Marshall has always been a friend and still remains a friend of mine. Friend to the end. Looking at the bright side of it all, I don't know if Marshall knows it or not, but Marshall you have challenged me to be a better me. Because I've seen the champion in you challenges me to continue to keep my head up. Marshall I am truly proud of you and all of your accomplishments.

Moreover, another bright side of my story is I know that my mother is watching from heaven. I believe that she is in heaven and smiling down on me. She knew that she was a blessing and a part of the history of Marshall's success. For me, my mother was not here to witness my life change, but I made it. I think that would have been all she wanted. She wanted me to be the person I was intended to be and finally reaching a point of success in my life. This is what she wanted and had hoped and prayed for. She never gave up on me, therefore I could not give up on myself. Knowing what my mother did for me and for Marshall was not in vain. Many people did not know it, but Marshall never stopped caring for my mother. He took care of my mother until her dying day. What a way to repay someone. May she rest in peace, my mother (Ms. Sibby).

Furthermore, audience this book has played a therapeutic role in my life. I am so happy that I have had the opportunity to share my experiences with you guys. I'm not only writing this book in hope of helping somebody, but to be honest this book has helped me to overcome. You can't imagine how much I have been helped by sharing these experiences with the world. This book has helped me to better understand myself. It has helped me to open up and understand myself, vent my feelings and give myself a voice. This book has helped me see the bright side of my life. This book is written as a personal sacrifice to help people who are in my position, not make the mistakes that I made. I hope this book serves as a map to help navigate your life. It might help the younger generation to get a better perspective about the sports world.

To the younger generation seeking careers in sports

In the current state of the sports world, the contracts that are offered to the youth based on their abilities and skills as sportsman are astronomical. When making decisions about the future it is important to surround yourself with someone who is familiar with you and your situation. Therefore it is important for the younger generation to consider how important it is to have the right people who will help to make the best decisions that reflect their goals and aspirations.

This book may also help the younger generation have an easier transition into adulthood. Especially, coming of age as an African American Male in today's society. I challenge the younger generation to evaluate what one might call a friend. Some friends are there for seasons in your life, others for the long haul. Evaluate who is real and who is not truly a friend. It has been said that friends come a dime a dozen. True friends come once in a life time. Value your friendships and relationships, because through those voices one can get the kind of counsel that you need when make those life altering decisions. These voices will be the voices of truth that counsel you based on your best interests.

Further Guidance for the Youth: A voice and a spirit of Truth

To the young generation, I ask that after reading this book you take heed to and consider the things I've discussed in this book. Believe it or not, I was once young. I lacked knowledge and was blind to the facts of life. I hope my story inspires and encourages you to make better decisions for your life. I hope that you learn from what I've experienced and you find comfort in knowing that you do not have to go through the same experiences I went through. You can make better choices. I would like to call attention to what I spoke about in Chapter 2 and how the hood can rob you of your potential. You have to be careful to choose correctly the kind of life you want to have in your adult years. Growing up in an environment that are riddled with crime, violence and even unemployment, can play a role in destroying who you can be. You have to take the necessary steps to avoid detours to your life by making good choices. Friendships are important in making those decisions. The hood has a way of making you what statistics says you will be. The hood has a way of molding you into what it says you should be, so you must take charge. I want you to know that the so called negative energy that we use to so call prosper or come up, can also be channeled into something positive.

Let's discuss for instance someone who sells illegal drugs. In order to keep up with this profession, he must be able to calculate sales, profit margin and likelihood of repeat customers. In a profession related to money these are the same skills needed in trading stocks and bonds, skills of an accountant among other professions. This person is demonstrating that he has potential to function in society in a number of professions. Take for instance Master P. He is someone whom I admire and highly respect. I respect him not because he is rich, but he used his knowledge of the streets and his environment and integrated that into the business world. He built an empire. He demonstrated that we can't use the excuse of being from an impoverished environment as something that can hold you back. I know that this is a fact because he was from an impoverished area. He was from what is known as the Calliope Housing Projects. He took what he knew about the streets and turned it into a real business venture. He knew what people wanted and what they were looking for and he fulfilled what they needed. He is one of the richest men in our society. He found his gifting, talents, skills and brilliance and tapped into all of his potential. He turned his whole life around in a positive manner. He is the CEO of all types of businesses and networks. He is a true inspiration.

Let's take another character from the hood, he portrays himself as a con man. He uses what he knows people want; their desire to prosper. He engages them in some kind of game. While playing this game he may make a potential client believe that he or she has a good chance of winning the game in hopes of winning money. He knows that it is just a trick for the person to get involved and at the right moment they will lose everything that they have and what they had already won in a previous game. Instead of deceiving people this person can really find ways to help people and instead of giving them false hope he can give them hope that is real. This is something that a preacher of the gospel does. He influences people using the word of God that there is hope. The con man can use his influence and intuitiveness to persuade people in real hope. These are gifts and skills that this person has and therefore can be used in a more positive arena.

Yet there is another character we can learn from, the so called pimp. He is another person that uses what he knows about people to take advantage of them. He knows that women may have issues with their self esteem. He may persuade the woman that she is loved by him and that they are family. She feels acceptance where there had been no acceptance, she may not have had a family. He wins her over. Instead of him destroying her mind and capitalizing from her insecurities. She may think that this is the only thing she is good for. Just imagine if he would use his influence to build her up instead of tearing her down. He could be the family she has never had. He could be her provider, comforter, companion, lover and friend and everything that a husband is to a woman. He could even use this power and potential he possesses and be a counselor for runaways, consultant or even a life coach. There are many possibilities alternatives, and scenarios.

Young people please take the time to realize just how much more you are and are valued. You are tomorrow's future. Don't let your negative situation and circumstances overtake you to the point where you believe that there is nothing

more that life can offer other than what is around you. Don't believe this misconception. It is possible to create the kind of world that you want. Life has a lot to offer just put your mind to what it is that you want. There are many opportunities for you to discover the potential that is on the inside of you. This is a Wake-Up Call. Please use your God given talents and gifts while you are young. If I can do it, if Marshall can do it, if Master P. can do it, then ask yourself the question, why can't I?

THANKS TO THE READERS

Now that I've finished telling my story, I would like to analyze what I have done. I would first like to thank everyone who has taken the time to purchase and read my book. I would like to thank you for your time. I would like you the reader know that this experience has been truly a blessing to me. This book has allowed me to share my story, inspire others and get this book out to the world. I want you the reader to know that I needed to get this story out of my being. Writing this book has helped me to deal with a lot of unanswered questions about my life. A lot of things were truly confusing to me at one time. This experience of being the best friend of someone of Marshall Faulk's stature is no ordinary situation. There are not many people you can go to for guidance in this situation. I had to share this story with the world. Those who knew us both know the intricate details of our beginnings. This book has help those people better understand how things between Marshall and I ended up. This story and all that I went through was a real life situation and will go down in history as a part of history. My story had to be shared because it is the missing piece of the puzzle that needed to be shared. This piece was missing and it was lost. To God be the glory the piece of the puzzle has been completed. God knew where the missing piece was all the while. Since that piece has been found it is time to connect that part so that the full image can be seen and its meaning known. I'd like to thank the world for allowing me to express my deepest thoughts and giving me a voice that was once silenced by society. Greater is he that is in me than he that is in the world. I am more than a conqueror I am Mark Bruno author of Living in the Shadow of being the best friend of Marshall Faulk Hall of Fame Inductee (New King James Bible, Romans 8).

FINAL THOUGHTS

I never thought that one day that I would write a book. I am an author. I never imagined that this could happen. I never thought my trials, tribulations and pain would be such an aspiration in my life. I never thought that I would have the opportunity to share my experiences in a book. Now I know my experience with my friend Marshall and the times we shared and all that we have been through was some meaningful times. I always thought that it was a trip living a life of a millionaire. I thought that that was the high light of my life. I thought all of those experiences were the high points of my life, the good times, the money, and everything that went along with that life. My writing this book and discovering this talent within me as a writer and story teller was a real mind blowing experience. I surprised myself when I dug deep and found the courage, ability and the strength to start this endeavor and see its completion. This has brought true inner peace and confirmation to all my unanswered questions and doubts about why all of this happened in my life. The real truth of the matter is that some things had to happen for the final outcome to be as real as it is. I am now an author and I have so many stories to tell and books to write. Look out world. Author and writer Mark Bruno has found his claim to fame.

ANALYSIS

As far as Marshall is concerned, I as his friend should have took the time out to realize what a great responsibility my friend was facing. Now that I look at it, I can imagine now what a big mountain of adversity Marshall probably had to face. As a friend walking with Marshall alongside him through his journey of success it never crossed my mind before writing this book, the load and responsibility he carried. He had a lot of pressure. He was a multi-millionaire at the age of 22. That was a lot to face. Imagine being that young and having the world and anything in it. Sounds good, but there is a price he had to pay. I realize through this journey and experiences I learned that money is not everything. It's not the pure root of happiness to make your life happy. Don't get me wrong, having money is a blessing. If you have it and God in your life then it's a blessing. If it is earned in the right way that should definitely be a source of gratitude. As Marshall's friend I remember a time in his life when he was unhappy because he thought that he was unworthy of the blessing that God blessed him with. Looking back, I now realize that money isn't everything. He had money, houses, clothes, cars and any and everything you could wish. He had everything one could want and there were still periods where he was unhappy, something was still missing.

When I look back I realize we still had a lot to learn about success and money. I now realize his position and now understand a little better where he might be coming from. Only God knows all of the details to this scenario. I sincerely hope throughout Marshall's success and achievements he has given God the glory for those things. This is truly where everything comes from. Who am I to judge? I share these things in my book because, the bible says that the devil comes to kill, steal and destroy (New King James Bible, 2010). I share these things because I wouldn't want the next person to go through what I went through. I would like to see this cycle broken. The issues that Marshall and I faced could be resolved easier if you have the knowledge to do so. I wrote this book to address these types of issues. Where I came from, we were taught and raised in love and were expected to love one another. Even though we grew up in a bad environment, we still had good people around us and we were taught right from wrong. So I'm taking a stand and as a sacrifice to you all, sharing my story. I am giving voice to anyone who has ever experienced what I am going through. I am bringing light to a situation that many don't talk about. I am informing my fellow brothers who will one day possess fame, fortune, success, and reach celebrity status of the responsibility that they will have in the lives of those around them. I am specifically speaking of those that helped them to get to where they are. We all have some effect on each other's lives. If someone is close to you, then they make some kind of difference in your life. As I've stated earlier everybody's situation is different, but I believe my story mirrors the story of a lot of people in many different situations. This is another reason that I have written this book. I know people have gone through this, but I have never heard of a book about. Let me be the first. I will simply go down in history for doing so. Since I've been in this situation I am now an expert on the subject. I am here writing this book through inspiration that was given to me by God. Actually, I am glad to be first and bring awareness to this situation and give voice to those who have suffered as I have. I know that things should not have turned out the way they did. This is not the way things are supposed to be. This is not the way things are supposed to be between friends.

On the other hand, I'm glad called on me to bring awareness to my fellow brothers. I thank him for choosing me and giving me the knowledge and wisdom to send out a message to the world and my fellow brothers. They might have unknowingly, in the height of success and fame done the same thing to their friends and maybe even family members. Man I'm making an appeal to you not to forget those who call you friend. That is a painful situation for anyone to have to go through. This situation could make you or break you, but it definitely will show you what's inside of you. I'm glad that I was from the Ninth Ward and I was in the school of "hard knocks." If not I don't know how I would have bounced back from it all. I was built to survive, built to overcome, and most of all built to take a lick, built to make a dollar, built to fall down and dust myself off and get back up. On the real, everybody's not built to make. Some people don't have that drive.

Moreover, I would like to congratulate my brothers who made it. Who made it out of bad environments, bad family backgrounds and just who overcame impossible situations, you are to be commended. All I ask is that you don't forget those who are still at the bottom, striving to make it. I'm here to tell you to be mindful of those people who watched you succeed, because those are the very people who will be there when you fall. If they loved you in the beginning, they will love you when you whether or not you have fame and success. This is just a message. I'm trying to keep it all as real as I can. This is a big universe and we all have a divine purpose. Believe it or not we all affect the lives of others. Let's connect the dots and stop getting in each other's way. Let's put the pieces back that are the broken pieces of each other's lives. To my brothers and to whom this may concern, be the role models that make people want to be like you. You matter to the younger generation, because they are watching. You have a responsibility being in such a high position. The bible says, to whom much is given, much is required (New King James Bible, 2010). Make it possible for those who come behind you to reach success. Help the less fortunate, give back like those who gave to you and who made it possible for your success. This can include struggling communities, speaking to students in economically disadvantaged schools, give to those who might make a difference one day.

WHERE ARE THEY NOW?

As a reflection on our childhood, I am amazed at how everyone's life turned out. My circle of friends like George, Marshall, myself and Courtney; amazing to see how we each had a path in life to take. We all took different paths in our life and we are all shocked and surprised at the paths we all took. We would have never expected to be, not in our wildest dreams. I'm truly grateful and thankful of how everyone in my click is still alive. They are all living a good life and doing well. Mark Bruno, a cook and new found author. Glory be to God for his mercy. My boy George Elpheage, when I say this it gives me chills and fills me with God's spirit, that George is a minister of the gospel, a preacher. I am so glad that our friendship is still true. Lil Courtney, better known as Cotto Cash is now a grown man and a true entrepreneur and business owner. Still with the hustle we planted in him. Now he uses what he knows and learned in a good way. He now owns a tire shop and has a car lot where he sells used cars. Glory be given to God for that. Last but not least, Marshall Faulk. Well what can I say? Most valuable player retired from the NFL, Hall of Fame Inductee, Husband and Father. When I think about this and those words coming out of my mouth, I am truly proud of him; to have been there to witness him along this journey.

Knowing that I was a part of his success truly blows my mind. I know deep down in my heart all I went through was not in vain. My experiences and trials and tribulations none was in vain and neither were our friendship a mistake. To God be given all of the Glory.

This is a special shout out in Loving Memory of Maurice Duncan Quarterback for George Washington Carver Rams. May he rest in peace. Maurice was killed and died of gun-shot wounds shortly before he was to graduate high school. I remember how the hood could take you under.

Marshall Faulk unveils his hall of fame trophy of himself.

Left to Right: Marshall Faulk, Agent Rocky Arceneaux

Mark Bruno Author of "Living in the Shadow".

FINAL WORD

I hope after reading this book I've touched the hearts of people. Not only the ones that I know personally, but hopefully I've touched the world by bringing forth my story, message and all that I've learned through this journey. Much love and much hope and power to the lost and found. Thank you all. Remember to keep your head up through all your difficulties and know that it's not over as long as you have breath in your body.

ACKNOWLEDGEMENTS

First on my list before everybody is my big brother Anthony Lewis. Man you just don't know how much you've meant to me. I thank you for being a true brother and friend, during times of need despair and struggles. I thank you always being there for me, always believing in me, and always encouraging me and I mean always. Man words can't even express my gratitude for the person that you are. I'm glad God used you to be a part of my life. Dog! You are truly an angel in disguise. I Love you. My big brother, Anto from the N.O., Baby.

My slick side big brother and some might don't know just how close we are and our history as sincere friends. Shout out to my other big brother and true inspiration of what a friend is. My dude Shawn Pepp. Keep up the good work. Role model material . . . . I see ya, baby. Thanks for never doubting me and judging me, and thanks for always keeping it real.

To my brother from another mother who has always been a true friend and mentor, and who has always wanted the best for me and one who I've always had the most utmost respect for. It is none other than my brother and friend Tyrone Williams aka Cussy. Dog I like to thank you for never giving up on me, I'd like to thank you for always keeping it real with me and sharing things with me from a different aspect that I couldn't otherwise see. You showed me how to look at the situation I was dealing with between Marshall and myself. I want you to know your words and inspiration were not in vain. I finally see the light Cussy. You will forever be my dog. Thanks for always being in my corner. There's none like you . . . . true friend indeed. Hope I made you proud . . . . I finally did it, I wrote the book . . . I know after reading it, you will love it. Thanks big bro, the sky is the limit for us. This is only the beginning. You know I got more stories to tell and more books to write. You're next up to bat. Should I say comedy central? Dreams do come true. Look at me glory be to God.

To cousin Joe Magee, haven't talk to you for a while, but I want you to know that you've always been one of the many that I've looked up to and shared a special bond with. You're not only my blood, but you've always been a true friend in encouraging me in any situation. There are things that I'll never forget. You know our history. Joe you know they can't keep us good brothers down. Love ya boy. Keep ya head up. Hope I made you proud. It is what it is.

Now how can I tackle this acknowledgement? My sister Monique Bruno, I love you baby. I'd like to thank you for not excepting the person I had become through that dark stage of my life and you knew that it wasn't me. All the while I thought you didn't love your big brother anymore. The reality of it all was that you knew I was better than what I had become. On the flip side, you never truly turn your back on me and you always came with that unconditional love. I love you so much. Let's continue to make momma proud of us. Smooches Bruno family, the sky is the limit (no ceiling).

To my boy George Elpheage . . . .Dog it's been a hallelujah journey. I want to thank you for always being my ride or die brother. I want to thank you for the times we shared in our younger days as friends. We've learned a lot together and experienced a lot together. If only people knew. They couldn't walk a mile in our shoes. I want you to know you've always been a significant part of my coming of age to be the man I am today. You always will be a part of me my brother and true friend. I am so proud of the man you've become, Minister Elpheage. Thank you Lord. George I now can see the light big brother. God is so good. Thank you my friend for letting your light shine and being another example of the glory of God. Ninth ward soldier until the end.

To a person I must acknowledge a true friend that cross my path in life, none other than Mark Reese (aka Big Mimzie). I can't forget about ya dog. Mark you were a true friend indeed. Thanks for all you've done and thanks for being a real friend in those times and in those days.

To one of my brothers for life, none other than Milton Clark (aka silk). Well dog what can I say? You know our journey, you know our experiences as friends. I can't even express in words, you already know the deal. Love ya man. You are more than a conqueror; you are one of the realest in my eyesight. I know you are proud of me after reading this book. I hope it makes a difference after reading it. I hope it impacts your life. We will always be friends until the end. Holler if you hear me.

To my family, the Louisa Street Posse, I want to thank all of y'all for not excepting the person I had become through that dark stage

in my life. I just want to thank y'all for the tough love . . . .
. .and I mean tough love. No hard feelings, you all are my family
and love conquers all, don't forget that. To all my aunts, uncles and
cousins who have always been a part of my life and upbringing, I love
you all to the fullest. Look at me now. As stated by the great Mayou
Angelou, "still I rise."(1970)

This acknowledgement may seem kind of strange, but it's true.
I like to thank my ex-wife Mera Bercy Bruno for not accepting the
person I had become as well. Even though things did not work out
for the better between us, I still would like to thank you. My exit
out of your life has forced and challenged me to be a better man.
Especially for our kids I say thank you . . . . Makera, Markyra,
Marko, daddy love y'all. Daddy also loves Dominique Bruno and
Mark Bruno Jr. Never forget your daddy loves you.

Last but not least, I can't forget my auntie Delores Magee you
are a true inspiration to me. You are an example of what a family's
mindset of love for one another should be. You are a strong black
queen, you are a soldier of love, you are a Soul survivor. Your love
and ambition of family unity is broader than what the world may
not know about you. Don't let things and certain situations and
circumstances change that about you. I'm here to tell you as your
nephew you're one of the greatest aunts in the world. You are a loving
and caring person. I just thought you should know. Thanks for being
there for me in my times of despair. I hope you're proud of me, well I
know you are (Smile). R. I. P. gramps I know she is smiling down.

One more, I must acknowledge my aunt Diane Joseph aka Teedie. Well Teedie what can I say? I guess I can say back in stride again. (smile have a laugh on me).

To all of my real peers, the people I grew up with. I want to give you guys a shout out. If I forget anyone please forgive me and know that you are included.

Taurus Horn	Benny Washington (R.I.P.)	Dewayne Miller
Kwesci Howard	Burnell Watson(fat)	Gerald Preston
Larry Howard	Darnell Watson	Teeky
Corey Horne	Walter Sterling(Poo-man)	Eric Narcisse
Gennaro Pen	Bobby Roy	Mason Lavigne
Tremell Jackson	Derrick Evans	Brian Coleman
Jerome McNeil	Larry Howard	Trish
Nakia Gaines	James Miller	Keith Barres
Kevin Barres	Thelmas Finnie	
Cedric Winguard	Danny Wallace	
Lacrease	Willie McGuire	
Johnny Parker		
Walleed Matthews		
William O'neal		
John Porter		
Dirty Red		
Keith Bundy		
Ronald Price		
Lamont Matthews (flute)		
Darryl Henderson(Snott Box)		

Marquette Watts(Bird)

Earl Hunter

Lyndell Johnson(Baldy)

Lowell Johnson

Kirk Stewart

George Angeletti

Eugene Toney(Deanie)

Troy Porter

MY CLOSURE TO IT ALL

I couldn't close this book without these special thanks to these three people that I couldn't have done this without.

First on the list is my brother and friend Marshall Faulk. Dog even though things are not the same and a lot has changed in our lives since the days of us growing up and experiences all we have together throughout our coming of age. I just want to thank you for the ride and the experiences along the way. Man I've learned a lot about a lot of things as you can see in the book. I want to thank you for the adversity and I want to thank you for always being a friend. Believe it or not you are still being a friend to me by showing me tough love. I want to thank you for allowing me to fly and take wings to find my way again. I want you to know there are no hard feelings. I thank you my brother and I wish you much more success. Believe it or not I am so proud of you dog. Thanks for making me challenge who I am. Ha, Ha, Ha, you know one thing about me Marshall, I am a Soldier Boy! Isn't that brilliant of me huh? I know you like the book. This book is one in a million. Greenlight!

This person here I'd like to give a special, special thanks to and this person is none other than my baby and dearest friend Rhonda Hutchinson. Well baby, what can I say we did it. Rhonda I'd like to thank you so much for believing in me, for loving me, for dealing with me, and never giving up on me. I'd also like to thank you for always being there for me especially being there with me hands on helping me with my book and collaborating on my story. I want you to know you are truly an angel of mine and I'm blessed to have you in my life. You know the sky is the limit baby. Rhonda Hutchinson aka Diamond a woman that wears many hats(smile). Can you believe we did it. Can I say next up to bat.

Last and they say you save the best for last. My mother, Ms. Sibby may she rest in peace. Thank you so much for your unconditional Love you gave us. It has given me the strength in my heart to survive and overcome life trials like you would've wanted me to. I love and miss you. Hope this made you proud. Well I know it has made you proud. Finally out of the shadow. I am now my own man mamma. Blessed and highly favored.

RESOURCE LIST

Hinton,M. (2011). Marshall Faulk's Journey to Canton. *The Times Picayune.* Photo courtesy of Times Picayune Magazine.

McClurkin,D. (2000). We fall down. *Live from London.* Album Verity Records.

Merriam Webster's Collegiate dictionary (11th edition)(2010). Springfield, MA: Merriam-Webster.

Wright, B.(1988). No Pain, No Gain. *Mother Wit.* Album. Miss B. Records.

Mark Bruno/Author/Entrepreneur

Mark Bruno was born in New Orleans,La. He was raised in the Ninth Ward and attended George W. Carver High School. He became friends with Marshall Faulk during the early years of his childhood. He was inspired to write a book about his experiences as Marshall's best friend. Throughout his life's journey he discovered he wanted to write about experiences and the lives of others. He then became an author. Once he tapped into his brilliance a gift for writing he discovered he had a lot of stories to tell.